A DURYEE

by
Thomas P. Southwick

New Foreword by
Thomas S. Southwick

Introduction by
Brian C. Pohanka

Patrick A. Schroeder Publications
Brookneal, VA 24528

Introduction and New Materials By Brian C. Pohanka in
Collaboration with Patrick A. Schroeder

Copyright © 1995 For All New Materials
By Brian C. Pohanka & Patrick A. Schroeder
All Rights Reserved

Cover: The 5th New York at Gaines's Mill by Keith Rocco 1991.
Courtesy of Tradition Studios, Woodstock, VA.

Cover Design: Patrick A. Schroeder

Published By
Patrick A. Schroeder Publications
Rt. 2, Box 128
Brookneal, VA 24528

Printed in the United States by
Farmville Printing
Farmville, Virginia

ISBN-1-56190-086-9

FOREWORD

With the reprinting of <u>A Duryee Zouave</u>, I wish to pay tribute to the service of my great-grandfather, Sergeant Thomas P. Southwick of the Fifth New York. Not only for serving his country in the Civil War, but for taking the time to keep his diary, despite all the hardships he went through. I also would acknowledge my great-aunt, Elizabeth Southwick, who saw that her father's story was published.

Those of us who carry on the Southwick name know how fortunate we are. With my great-grandfather's company and regiment decimated in those terrible battles, it is truly a miracle that he survived. But because he lived to write this little book, perhaps he will always be remembered.

I especially want to thank the modern-day Fifth New York, the members of which do such a super job of keeping the name of Duryée's Zouaves alive. They, too, deserve recognition for seeing that my ancestor and his outfit are not forgotten.

Thomas S. Southwick
Edgewater, Maryland
September 19, 1995

INTRODUCTION

The stirring saga of the Civil War abounds with deeds of gallantry and willing sacrifice by units whose members were bonded together by mutual patriotism, a common cause, a shared idealism, and the ineffable brotherhood of arms. It was an all too tragic occurrence in that bloodiest of American conflicts for a regiment to lose fifty, sixty, even eighty percent of its number in a single day of battle. As that soulful scholar-turned-soldier Joshua Lawrence Chamberlain put it, "The muster-rolls on which the name and oath were written were pledges of honor,--redeemable at the gates of death. And they who went up to them, knowing this, are on the list of heroes." Even before the first battles were fought, many regimental commanders sought to strengthen their volunteers' sense of esprit de corps by adopting distinctive and often colorful uniforms. One such officer was Colonel Abram Duryée, a wealthy Manhattan businessman and respected veteran of the New York State Militia, who saw to it that his Fifth New York Volunteer Infantry was outfitted in the exotic regalia of the French Zouaves. Dozens of wartime units ultimately sported the braided jacket, baggy trousers and tasseled fez of those famed French colonial troops, and Zouave regiments served from Bull Run to Appomattox. But of all the American Zouaves, none attained a more exalted reputation for military bearing, proficiency of drill, and discipline under fire than Duryée's Fifth New York.

The flashy New Yorkers paid a price for their valor. In their two-year term of service, 489 of the 1500 men born on the rolls were killed, wounded or captured on the battlefields of Maryland and Virginia. Hundreds more found their health permanently undermined by the rigors of campaign, and the fever-ridden swamps of the Virginia Peninsula. But, as veteran Alfred Davenport noted in his 1879 regimental history, "there are none but are proud to say that they served in the 5th New York Zouaves."

Thomas P. Southwick, a 24-year-old employee of Manhattan's Third Avenue Railway Company, was among the first to join Duryée's Zouaves in the heady rush to the colors that followed the bombardment of Fort Sumter. On April 26, 1861, he joined the ranks of Captain Henry A. Swartwout's Company F, and began to learn the profession of arms in the regimental camp of instruction at Fort Schuyler.

While the Fifth New York was noted for the number of imposing physical specimens and college graduates serving in its ranks, Thomas Southwick lacked both physical stature and a formal education. Only 5'1" tall, and weighing less than 100 pounds, he was, in mid-19th century slang, a "pony." Born to a poor family, Thomas had been orphaned at an early age. The 1850 census shows Thomas and John Southwick -- presumably one of his brothers -- living on Randall's Island in a public facility providing what one New York City guidebook described as "nurseries for the support and instruction of destitute children." Eventually moving in with a married sister, Thomas worked as a newsboy before obtaining employment with the railway company.

That Southwick was able to avoid the potential pitfalls of his Dickensian childhood was due in large part to his abiding love of books. A voracious reader, he took particular delight in the works of Shakespeare, and indulged his interest by attending frequent performances of the Bard's dramas at Manhattan theaters. His reading included not only novels -- with Dickens an obvious favorite -- but the works of antiquity, and he was even able to pick up a smattering of Latin.

Clearly Thomas Southwick was no ordinary young man, and it is not surprising that he made an excellent soldier. Except for one lapse, when he ran the guard at the Zouaves' camp in Baltimore to visit some young ladies and attend a play -- an infraction that saw him confined briefly in the regimental guardhouse at Fort Federal Hill -- his was an admirable record indeed. When the Fifth was mustered out in May of 1863, Thomas Southwick proudly bore the chevrons of F Company's Fourth Sergeant.

Given the terrible loss of life incurred by the Fifth New York in their two years of war, Southwick was fortunate to emerge from his experiences unscathed. He witnessed first-hand the clash at Big Bethel and the slaughter of Gaines's Mill, that bloodiest battle of the Seven Days in which the Zouaves lost a third of their number. He endured the nerve-wracking tension and threat of imminent death in the ravaged streets of Fredericksburg, as the Fifth helped cover the retreat of Burnside's stricken army, and battled amidst the tangled wilderness at Chancellorsville. And though many of his comrades fell prey to sickness and disease, Southwick experienced good health throughout his term of service.

It is likely that Southwick's memoirs would have been lost to history had he been present with the Fifth New York at the Second Battle of Bull Run. August 30, 1862 was the most tragic day in the unit's history; as Zouave Andrew Coats aptly put it, "where the regiment stood that day was the very vortex of hell." Of some 500 men who attempted to stave off Confederate General James Longstreet's massive onslaught, 325 fell in a scant eight minutes time -- 120 of them dead or dying. Having been placed in charge of a detail escorting the regimental knapsacks from the Peninsula to Washington, Southwick returned to Company F to find a mere handful of survivors -- so few in fact, that D and F companies had been temporarily merged to form a composite company only 17 strong.

From the pages of his diary, which he carried to war along with a much-thumbed volume of Shakespeare, Southwick appears to have kept his sense of optimism, rarely grumbling or bemoaning his fate as soldiers are often wont to do. "Pony" was a popular figure in the regiment, and frequently called upon to entertain his comrades with dramatic readings and theatrical burlesques. He was a philosopher, possessing a love of nature as well as a healthy sense of irony, and his characterizations of officers and fellow enlisted men are perceptive and succinct. None of these traits were lost when, late in life, he began to rework his diary for publication.

Southwick pokes gentle fun at his innocent dreams of glory, before he had "seen the elephant" -- soldier parlance for the baptism of fire. "I'd be a hero of course," he wrote, "if there were any Confederate flags to tear down or great generals to rescue. I'd be just the boy to do it." War's grim realities soon put an end to those delusions, and Southwick was not one to shy away from a recounting of battlefield horrors. Typical is his description of a stricken Confederate soldier: "part of his head had been blown away," Southwick writes, "and his quivering brain was exposed."

By the time of his muster-out in May 1863, Thomas Southwick had experienced his share of hardship, and had his fill of death and carnage. Though the war was far from over, like most of the Fifth's surviving two-year men he had no desire to re-enlist in another regiment. When Colonel Cleveland Winslow attempted to reorganize the Duryée Zouaves as the Fifth New York Veteran Volunteer Infantry, only a handful of the "Old Fifth" responded to his call. Having raised only four companies, Winslow returned to the front as commander of a battalion that while clad in Zouave finery, was in fact the Fifth New York in name only.

Southwick resumed his job with the Third Avenue Railway as a car painter, and on March 17, 1864, he married 20-year-old Helen Graham at Manhattan's Seventh Street Methodist Episcopal Church. Their first child, Walter G. Southwick, was born in January of the following year, and in 1868 the family moved to Washington, D.C., where Thomas was employed as a painter for a streetcar manufactory. For the next two decades the Southwicks lived in a frame house at 229 8th Street, S.E., not far from Capitol Hill. Frances H. Southwick was born in Washington in 1869, and a third child, Elizabeth M. Southwick, on June 8, 1871.

Distance precluded Thomas Southwick from attending the meetings of the Manhattan-based Fifth New York Veterans Association, but he did join the Grand Army of the Republic and was an active member of the Masonic Fraternity. He remained an avid reader and theater-goer, and passed his enthusiasm for the stage on to his son, who preserved the playbills of dozens of performances the two attended.

Like so many old soldiers, the legacy of Thomas Southwick's wartime service proved a mixed blessing -- pride in having fought in the ranks of a gallant command, coupled with increasing physical disabilities. When he applied for a pension in 1890, Southwick was still a "pony," standing only an inch over five feet, and weighing a mere 105 pounds. He suffered from chronic nephritis -- a disease of the kidneys -- as well as inflammation of the bladder and prostate. He wore a truss, and was almost totally deaf in his right ear.

Sensing that his days were numbered, Southwick began to transcribe his fading wartime diary into a bound ledgerbook, reworking his insightful but often brief entries into a more literary and readable format. His work was not yet completed when he succumbed to "chronic debility," caused by his kidney ailment, on April 12, 1892. His funeral was held at Washington's Second Baptist Church at 4th Street and Virginia Avenue, S.E., and he was buried with Masonic honors in the Capital's historic Congressional Cemetery.

In the years following Thomas Southwick's death, his widow Helen -- who outlived her husband by 22 years -- and daughter Elizabeth moved in with Frances and her husband James C. Maddox, a clerk at the Treasury Department. It was a large household -- the Maddox family included three sons and four daughters -- and with Walter Southwick busy raising his own family, the duty of completing Thomas Southwick's Civil War memoirs fell to his unmarried daughter, Elizabeth. Motivated, as she put it, "to preserve the record for his descendants," Elizabeth published A Duryee Zouave in 1930. She died August 4, 1942, at her sister's home, and was buried beside her parents in Congressional Cemetery.

It is hoped that this reprinting of Elizabeth Southwick's rare limited edition of her father's story will serve as a tribute to a brave soldier and a good man, and to keep alive the heroic legacy of the Duryée Zouaves. As Thomas Southwick's beloved Shakespeare wrote, "...they have us'd their dearest action in the tented field."

Brian C. Pohanka
Alexandria, Virginia

A Duryee Zouave

By Thomas P. Southwick

New Materials
Table of Contents

I. Foreword by Great-Grandson Thomas S. Southwick

II. Introduction by Brian C. Pohanka

III. Biographical Sketches .... p. 125

IV. Index to Southwick's Manuscript .... p. 140

Photographs

1. Thomas P. Southwick .... p. 4
2. The 5th New York Marching Down Broadway .... p. 8
3. Abram Duryée ....p. 22
4. The 5th New York at Camp Hamilton .... p. 40
5. Non-Commissioned Staff Mess .... p. 46
6. Bayonet Exercise .... p. 49
7. Colonel Gouverneur Kemble Warren .... p. 81
8. Lieutenant Colonel Hiram Duryea .... p. 81
9. Major Carlile Boyd .... p. 89
10. The 5th New York Monument .... p. 90
11. Double-quick .... p. 94
12. An Unknown Zouave at Falmouth .... p. 99
13. Officers at the Segar House .... p. 120
14. Operation on a "Wounded" Zouave .... p. 120
15. Rev. Dr. Gordon Winslow .... p. 121
16. Captain Judson Kilpatrick .... p. 121
17. Drilling at Fort Monroe .... p. 121
18. Charge at Big Bethel .... p. 122
19. Captain Cleveland Winslow .... p. 122
20. Lieutenant Gordon Winslow, Jr. .... p. 122
21. Private Frederick G. Smart .... p. 123
22. Unidentified Zouave with a Sharps Rifle .... p. 123
23. Lieutenant Thomas W. Cartwright .... p. 124
24. Captain George L. Guthrie .... p. 124
25. Sergeant George W. Wannemacher .... Back Cover

Thomas P. Southwick

A Duryee Zouave

—— by ——

Thomas P. Southwick

of

The Fifth New York Volunteers

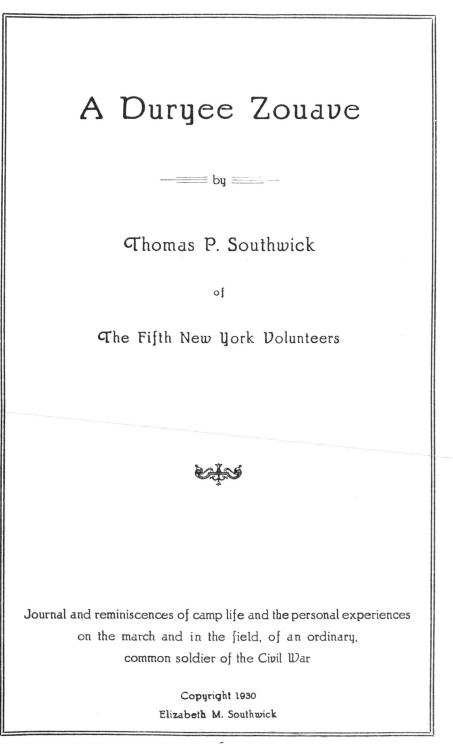

Journal and reminiscences of camp life and the personal experiences
on the march and in the field, of an ordinary,
common soldier of the Civil War

Copyright 1930
Elizabeth M. Southwick

Foreword

The early life of the Author was spent in the city of his birth, New York. When only twelve years of age, both parents having passed away, leaving a large family of children, of whom he was one of the youngest, and being thrown upon his own resources, he became a newsboy and made his home with an older sister. Having to make his living at this early age he had no opportunity to secure an education, but being ambitious he, by extensive reading and with determination acquired one himself.

The following narrative was prepared by him while serving with the Army of the Potomac, during the Civil War. During the latter days of his life, he was engaged in copying the record from the original diary, which was becoming faded and dim, but ere he could finish the task, the bugle call summoned him home and he laid down his pen, leaving the remainder to be completed by his children.

The original diary and the copy of Shakespeare which he carried through the entire two years of his service, are still in the possession of his family. The former is becoming obliterated with age and in order to preserve the record for his descendants is the purpose of this printed volume.

The Author makes no mention in his memoirs of a part he took in the campfire entertainments, but his ability to quote passage after passage of his beloved Shakespeare was soon discovered by his comrades who often invited him to render some selection, thus helping to enliven the dull monotony of camp life.

Several imposing monuments have been erected to the Fifth Regiment, New York Volunteers. Beside the one at Bull Run, of which there is a descriptive note, following the chapter on the second battle there, another fine shaft has been placed in the cemetery on Marye's Heights, Fredericksburg, and another at Gettysburg. On each one is conspicuously displayed the corps badge, the Maltese Cross.

E. M. S.

INDEX

CHAPTERS   PAGE

1. In which I manifest a taste for glory but decline to gratify it at the expense of my countrymen... 9

2. In which I experience a remarkable change of sentiment and resolve to gratify my taste for glory at the expense of the Southern Confederacy 11

3. In which I prove hard to please in choosing associates........................... 15

4. In which I am renamed, drilled and taken away............................... 18

5. In which I arrive at Fort Schuyler and get a taste of garrison life........ 23

6. In which I introduce the reader to several of my new acquaintances and we finally prepare to leave the Fort................................... 27

7. In which we break up housekeeping in Fort Schuyler and start for the war 31

8. Our arrival in Virginia... 34

9. Camp Hamilton 36

10. Picket duty 38

11. Battle of Big Bethel... 41

12. The First Battle of Bull Run.. 44

13. Federal Hill, Baltimore.. 47

14. Before Yorktown 50

15. On the march... 54

16. Camping near Hanover.. 58

17. Battle of Hanover Court House.. 60

18. Losses from disease.. 65

19. Review 68

20. A visit to the picket guard... 70

21. Battle of Gaines' Mill... 72

22. Battle of Malvern Hill.. 82

23. The Rebecca of Pottstown.. 86

24. The Second Battle of Bull Run... 88

25. Changes in Company F.. 91

26. Words of commendation; Review by General Hooker; Promised promotion 95

27. Fredericksburg 100

28. Christmas, eighteen sixty-two, and the New Year, in which I am discharged 115

7

The 5th New York marching down Broadway on their way to the front, May 23, 1861. [From a sketch by Frank Vizitelly]

CHAPTER I.

In which I manifest a taste for glory, but decline to gratify it at the expense of my countrymen.

Whether the love of glory is born in us, or whether we acquire it, I don't know; but it certainly exists, and manifests itself at an early period of our existence. When I was a child, the wonderful exploits of Jack-the-Giant-Killer, filled me with admiration. At Sunday School the stories of David and Goliath, and of Samson and the Philistines interested me, but when I grew older, heroes of the "stand and deliver" description supplanted the shepherd boy of Israel and the giant-killing Jack, and these in turn gave way to theatrical desperadoes like Macbeth, King Richard and other monsters of cruelty, brave enough, however, to bid their foes "lay on" and recklessly willing "to stand the hazard of the die." It was but a step from these to the demi-gods of Plutarch and demi-devils of Tacitus and eventually the perusal of war-like portions of history became my chief delight, and sometimes caused me to sigh for an opportunity to distinguish myself. I was enthusiastically fond of excitement and yet quite unwilling to become a voluntary martyr for the sake of posthumous fame. At any rate the cannon's mouth is not exactly the place where I should willingly have gone to "seek the bubble reputation."

For years the slavery question had been the "bone of contention" between the North and South and early in 1861 dire threatenings of war were being heard. Every country in the world manifests occasional symptoms of disorder and it doesn't require the brains of Shakespeare's "melancholy Dane" to discover "something rotten" in other states than Denmark, although I could hardly believe it about my own, and this rebellion was coming from the wrong direction. State after state went trotting out of the Union, money was appropriated for troops, mints and arsenals were seized, and people who never labored before, went diligently to work, drilling and digging in trenches. A rival establishment was set up in the South and we had a double-headed government with two chief magistrates. The people of South Carolina suddenly became a galaxy of shooting stars, putting a couple of ugly holes through the Star of the West which was bringing reinforcements to Fort Sumter, and the crippled Star was lying at anchor in the port of New York, while the Star shooters were devoting their attention to the Starry Banner that floated above the fort. Picks and shovels had been employed in the erection of batteries and they were discharging their big guns against the fort which the United States had built to protect them against a foreign foe. The people of the North acted as if stunned. They were indeed stupefied with amazement at the enormity of these outrages, but with singular pertinacity still clung to the idea there would be no war. "Oh, no, these people didn't really mean it. It was humiliating of course, for a legally elected President of the United States to be compelled to disguise himself in order to reach the Capital in safety, but these people would sooner or later be heartily ashamed of their actions."

CHAPTER 2.

*In which I experience a remarkable change
of sentiment, and resolve to gratify my taste
for glory at the expense of the Southern
Confederacy.*

One day, I think it was the first Sunday after the bloody tragedy in the streets of Baltimore, I was standing at the corner of Ann Street and Broadway, directly in front of Barnum's Museum, leaning carelessly against a post, watching the passersby. Behind me was the great showman's well-filled temple of curiosities, with his celebrated live lions stuffed with straw and his famous woolly horse and happy family of living animals, all natural enemies to each other, harmoniously dwelling together in a single cage. In front of me, on the opposite side of the street was a church, whose tall, graceful spire pointed toward the sky, and the substantial-looking Astor House with its big stores and handsome show windows extending along the square beyond. All the houses in every direction were gaily festooned with flags and streamers and from every window the Star-Spangled Banner proudly floated in the breeze, with its beautiful stripes and its deep blue field studded with bright stars to represent the states of our beloved country. Excited groups conversed together and on the breasts of nearly all, little knots of red, white and blue ribbon were conspicuously displayed. It was dangerous in some places to appear without it. "Show your colors" was the patriotic demand and those who neglected to do so were regarded with suspicion. The guns in South Carolina had aroused the people from their apathetic indifference and the blood shed in the streets of Baltimore had exasperated them to a degree of intensity almost bordering on frenzy. Millions of human beings, burning with indignation were now ready to uphold the flag that had been exposed to shot and shell, and the war fever pervaded the atmosphere and infected people of all classes from the rich merchant down to the bootblack who felt a desire to "polish off" the enemies of the old flag.

The President had called for troops and men were flocking to the recruiting offices in crowds to answer to the call. In the meantime militia regiments were hurrying to the defense of the Capital and "wars and rumors of wars" were heard throughout the land.

As I stood there I could hear the distant strains of martial music and soon a great crowd began to gather, as the head of the marching column appeared, and the cheers of the vast multitude, like a mighty roaring wave of sound, rolled down along the line. I never saw soldiers look as these soldiers did, there being a sober seriousness about them, and no one accustomed to the rollicking gayety and characteristic jauntiness of the citizen soldier would ever have supposed these solemn looking individuals belonged to the National Guard. The general impression was that the National Guard was "more ornamental than useful" but in emergencies like the present, when the regular standing army is too small and volunteers are too slow in learning the trade of war, or the art of killing people in a skillful and scientific manner, the National Guard becomes invaluable.

Up to this time the war fever had failed to produce any impression upon me. Once and once only during the long and bitter political campaign, sometime previous to this, did I believe there was any real danger and that was when Mr. William L. Yancey, the silver-tongued orator of the South, had the audacity to appear in the hall of Cooper Institute and deliver there one of the incendiary speeches with which he was endeavoring to fire the southern heart and prepare the way for secession. The extraordinary boldness of this man in predicting and advocating armed resistance against the government, in case the Republican Party succeeded in electing its candidate, irritated and exasperated even those friendly to the South. A tremendous crowd, made up of Union Democrats and Republicans, assembled in the hall to hear him and when he was introduced every eye was turned toward the platform as if they expected to see the great agitator appear in a blaze of red light and go skipping through the roof like a sky-rocket, but a sleek-headed, elegantly dressed gentleman in the rear, modestly advanced to the front platform. There was a feeble attempt to applaud, after which a storm of hisses greeted the silver-tongued orator. Mr. William L., however, was not of a retiring disposition. Firm as a rock he stood, the embodiment of composure. They finally got tired and the speaker in a clear voice said "I hope the time has not yet come when an American citizen from one section of the country cannot address his fellow-citizens in another, without the fear of being molested by his own countrymen." This little appeal for free speech had the desired effect, and he was allowed to proceed.

"The South," he said, "would never submit to the election of a sectional president. They would take up arms in their own defense. They would fight for their rights under the Constitution." The extraordinary nerve displayed and the earnestness with which he spoke made the situation seem alarming. Being at this time a red-hot Democrat, I never had the least idea that Abraham Lincoln would be elected. He was, though, and here was I a few weeks after his inauguration, witnessing the departure of a militia regiment to the war. They were a fine body of men, keeping step to the music of the band with heads erect, but their eyes were constantly wandering to the right or left for something dearer than discipline, sons for their parents, husbands for their wives and children, and young men for the "girls they were leaving behind them." Now and then someone would dart suddenly forward to hurriedly grasp the disengaged hand of some dear one in the ranks and then drop sadly back to gulp down the big sigh and repress, if possible, the rising tear.

I had resolved never to imbrue my hands in the blood of my countrymen, but these gallant fellows were my countrymen too, and surely nearer and dearer than those who were about to meet them in this unhappy conflict. The thought came with startling abruptness bringing with it some new ideas. A little coercion, after all might possibly be a very good thing if it would compel those hot-headed people to respect the old flag and obey the laws of the general government. What would they be to me if they were permitted to withdraw? Already they had severed their connection by withdrawing their senators and representatives. I had never thought this way before. It may have been the music,

13

"the ear-piercing fife and spirit-stirring drum" or the polished bayonets flashing in the bright sunlight. Could it be possible that I actually felt proud of these men who were going to butcher their fellow-countrymen? It certainly did seem so. How long under such reasoning could I possibly hope to remain neutral? And why should I hesitate to take sides even now? I found no difficulty taking part in the local contests of my early youth, in the desperate stone battles that we fought. It was sufficient for me to know that the antagonists were residents of another street. Even a street could be divided north and south or east and west. The unconquerable nature of our gang was plainly indicated by a war song of extraordinary strength and beauty although I was never able to clearly understand to what the first line of this remarkable couplet could possibly refer. We were not disposed to be critical, though, so we sang "The white cockade and the peacock feather, the seventeenth streeter will fight forever." While these thoughts were passing through my mind the band was playing and the troops were passing, some never to return.

There was something thrilling in the thought that these fine young fellows were going to battle bravely for what they believed to be right. It filled me with emotion, there was a flush in my cheeks that indicated a serious attack of military enthusiasm.

The people around me were cheering and clapping, and waving hats and handkerchiefs. Then in the middle of the battalion, the glorious old flag appeared with the bright stripes falling in graceful folds from the polished staff and I shouted and yelled until I was hoarse. Tears gushed into my eyes and I turned away firmly resolved to defend that flag against any that would raise their hands against it whether they were my countrymen or not.

CHAPTER 3.

In which I prove hard to please in choosing associates.

Having decided to enlist, I immediately began to look around for a suitable regiment. I think I wanted to find one composed entirely of gentlemen's sons, but I soon discovered there were none of that class, although there were gentlemen and gentlemen's sons in nearly every one. Company C of McChesney's regiment, Tenth New York Volunteers, was organized in the immediate vicinity of my residence, 55th Street and Third Avenue. It was under the command of Alec Elder, an experienced soldier who had seen service in the Mexican War. I knew him by sight and was slightly acquainted with some of the men, who like myself were employees of the Third Avenue Railway Company. These and many more were assembled in Winken's Brewery, where my brother Charlie, who also had caught the military fever, and myself signed our names to the list of future heroes.

Any one who supposes that the first installment of volunteers was taken exclusively from Sunday Schools and Temperance Societies is mistaken. They furnished their part, no doubt, but physical qualifications alone being necessary, naturally the most aggressive were the first to volunteer. This was the kind of people we found in Winken's Brewery enlivening the dullness of the occasion with a few personal shindies. I was not interested in dualistic brawls, although I spent four cents once, when a boy, for a little book entitled "How to Box" or the "Manly Art of Self Defence." It was a gem and would have been invaluable if it had only contained a few hints to beginners, not to begin at all; however, it taught me how to catch the blows on my wrists (before that I used to catch them all over my head). After I had studied it awhile I became confident in my ability to lick someone, and the opportunity soon presented itself in the shape of a strong, compactly built little Brooklyn dock loafer named Judy.

Judy was reading a theatrical poster, taking up most of the sidewalk, so I unhesitatingly brushed up against him. One glance at this ugly little customer's face, when he turned around, was enough to convince me that the staying qualities of the Seventeenth streeter were to be severely tested. After a slight struggle Judy was on the sidewalk and I was on top of him, for an accident ended the first round in my favor, for there was something slippery on the ground and Judy stepped on it. I magnanimously allowed him to get up, which was one of the mistakes of my lifetime. "Just you wait a minute," said he and darted down into a dingy basement under a gin mill and soon returned with a lot of others as rough as himself.

"Where is the fellow that wants to fight you, Judy?" said one, looking at me contemptuously, as if he thought it could not possibly be me. "Here I am," said I, quietly.

The battle, finally, after consultation, took place on a coal wharf. I don't know which of us led off, which drew the first blood or which obtained the first fall. It seemed to me I was falling all the time. Judy had no difficulty sending me down on the coal heap head first, sideways, backward and every other way until the ground was going around and my head was going around, and I was so dizzy I could scarcely stand up. Toward the last I began to gain on him a little, when I was treacherously struck down by one of his friends and kicked almost into insensibility. I heard some one cry "Police." Judy and his gang managed to get away, leaving me in possession of the field. The kind hearted guardian of the peace reprimanded me and permitted me to go. I had lost my hat and coat, some fragments of shirt, two or three handfuls of hair and a considerable quantity of blood. My experience in this battle of the coal wharf did not tend to diminish my previous dislike to personal encounters which were distasteful to me on the present occasion. Charlie, too, was displeased with his new associates so we took the first opportunity to withdraw.

The whole regiment had been ordered to assemble at the Mercer House the following day at ten o'clock and thither we repaired at the appointed time. There were about eight hundred men in the room, rough, hearty looking fellows, the very best material for soldiers, but not good for companions, especially when under the influence of John Barleycorn. Our tastes and inclinations were so different that Charlie startled me with the information that he, at least, couldn't stand it and intended to back out. He tried to persuade me to do the same, but I remained inflexible.

The next day I was obliged to go alone to headquarters and when I got there, had to remain whether I wanted to or not, for a man with a musket was stationed at the door to prevent anyone from leaving the room. I didn't like the idea of being penned up and wandered around the room like an entrapped rat looking for a way to escape and finally settled down Micawber-like for "something to turn up." Early in the afternoon we were marched to Washington parade ground and while resting after drill I made my escape. The next day we explored the city to find a regiment to our taste. In our perambulations we passed the old Bowery Theatre and Tammany Hall in each of which a regiment was organizing, the latter under the command of the renowned Jim Kerrigan and the former under the illustrious Billy Wilson. Jim's regiment didn't suit us at all, and Wilson's was entirely out of the question. After several days, Charlie, completely discouraged, gave up.

Finally, I resolved to join the first regiment that chance threw in my way and fortune favored me the next day and I became an enlisted soldier in Duryee's Zouaves, who were already quartered in Fort Schuyler and rapidly getting ready for the campaign.

Colonel Abram Duryee had been for many years commander of the far-famed Seventh Regiment, National Guards, and much of the praise bestowed upon that celebrated corps was justly due to him. He had no superior as a drill master and his reputation as a regimental commander was unequaled by that of any officer in the service of the state. I had never seen him, but his name was sufficient guarantee for the excellency of his men, and without a moment's hesitation I signed my name to the regimental roll and promised to be ready to report for duty the next day at twelve o'clock.

CHAPTER 4.

In which I am renamed, drilled and taken away.

While the city bells were vibrating in the ears of hungry thousands at twelve next day, I presented myself at the door, ascended the stairs and entered a large oblong hall, temporarily used as a recruiting office. About twenty or thirty recruits, as raw as myself, were already there, lounging lazily around the room, a dingy apartment formerly used for political purposes by the Lincoln and Hamlin Association of "Wide Awakes" in the exciting campaign of eighteen sixty. The names and pictures of the successful candidates had not yet been removed from the walls.

Some of the recruits were slowly pacing up and down the room in a deeply meditative mood, some staring at the homely features of the man on the wall who had been called to preside over the destinies of his country in its most trying emergency. I had never seen a more orderly and peacefully disposed set of individuals anywhere. They were thinking no doubt of the parting scenes of the morning, of their homes, friends, and firesides that some would never see again. I, too, had left loved ones behind, their sobs still ringing in my ears.

Each man was armed with a little bundle, mine containing several shirts and a volume of Shakespeare. I had taken the precaution of providing a high hat and of having an extra inch of heel added to my boots for fear of being rejected on account of my size. My friends caused this apprehension for they desired to know whether I was enlisting as a drummer or a powder monkey, therefore, I deliberately perpetrated a fraud on the government of the United States as outrageous as Barnum's woolly horse or the live lion stuffed with straw.

The fixtures of the room could be easily enumerated, two or three elevated desks, and long legged stools, a little round table and several arm chairs. A good natured officer was comfortably seated, calmly surveying the wreaths of curling smoke he was puffing from a cigar. He was elegantly attired in a new uniform of dark blue, ornamented with brass buttons and gold trimming. He was a contrast to the long-faced recruits.

About one o'clock the arrival of the surgeon, who was to decide upon our physical fitness, threw me into a cold perspiration and I shook with apprehension under his scrutinizing eye. If he had come to saw off a leg or an arm or remove our brains and scrub them, I couldn't have manifested much greater alarm and when we were ordered to "fall in for examination" I was so small and insignificant beside my comrades that I felt quite certain of being rejected and my heart palpitated so violently that I was afraid he would think I had heart disease. When I bared my bosom to his searching eye, I drew a long breath to expand it as much as possible. He seemed satisfied. He tapped me gently on the back and finally passed me with the remark, "You are what they call a pony," and this appeared so appropriate that I went by the name of "Pony Southwick" during the whole term of my service in the army of the United States.

After we had passed the examination of the surgeon, a tall, bony, hollow-cheeked individual commanded us to "fall in line" according to size. While we were doing this I was wondering who he was, and heard a young officer address him as Major Davis. I afterward ascertained that he was third in rank of regimental officers.

Major Davis was a man of few words and evidently was laboring under a severe cold and didn't care to waste his breath unnecessarily. He exercised us in facing, in filing right and left and in marching up and down the floor. When he became satisfied that we could walk without treading upon each other, he dismissed us saying he would conduct us to Fort Schuyler in a few minutes. I hadn't the least idea where Fort Schuyler was and would not betray my ignorance by asking. I got along remarkably well in the drill, there being no doubt about my position in the ranks, according to size, and there was nobody behind me to scrape the skin from my heels or endanger the durability of the extra inch of heel. My high hat, too, behaved itself better than I had expected.

About two o'clock in the afternoon we left the recruiting office, headed by the Major and marched solemnly down the "sixpenny side" of Broadway, a melancholy procession of patriots. It was a beautiful day and the great thoroughfare was thronged with all the different classes of the community. Every variety of shape and color was jumbled together from the pale faced American to the muscular, red faced Celt and charcoal colored Ethiopian. They called us the "awkward squad" and told us to "close up" and "keep step" which they seemed to consider very funny, while others desired to know how many rebels we expected to kill, plainly revealing by their levity, the terrible delusion that a large part of the North was still laboring under regarding the war. Few, even of the better informed, could properly appreciate the magnitude of the coming struggle. The odds were so heavily in our favor that there could be no serious resistance and the war would soon be over. The call for seventy-five thousand troops would frighten the South into submission.

When we reached Canal Street we were ordered to file left and down we went crossing the Bowery to one of those narrow and dirty streets on the East Side and then turning to the right we soon reached James slip where a handsome little steamboat, the Alice Price, was waiting to receive us. On our way down the men behaved themselves in a very orderly manner with the exception of one man who had been drinking.

Wreaths of dark smoke were rising from the smokestack when we approached and as we marched around the boxes and barrels crowded together on the dock the bell was ringing gaily, and the white steam escaping from the noisy pipe, indicated our speedy departure. Unhesitatingly we crossed the gang plank with a firm elastic step and with a martial air ascended the brass plated steps to the deck from which I could see my cousin's house in Brooklyn and even the windows of the room in which I had spent many pleasant hours. Memories were crowding upon me when the little vessel left the dock and started out into the stream. My mind was filled with melancholy thoughts for I feared I might never return to the city of my birth, now spread out like a panorama and slowly passing away. The gallant little vessel appeared to be instinct with life, bounding over the wavelets like a racer and seemed to breathe beneath our feet, but it was sad to think that every stroke of the paddle was taking me farther from home, farther from the place where I had learned to lisp the names of Father and Mother, who were now sleeping in the city churchyard, rather, where it used to be, but my brothers and sisters were thinking of me, and praying for my safe return. How little I knew until that day how much I loved them and how it distressed me to think I might never see them again. I had left them bravely as a soldier should, but it was extremely hard work and before they got through with me I could realize the truth and exclaim with the poet:

"Ye who have known what 'tis to dote upon
A few dear objects will in sadness feel
Such partings break the heart they fondly hope to heal."

There was a great deal of the Spartan spirit in our family and some of my relatives had no objection to my going to the war if I'd only keep out of danger, while others didn't think the success of either side was of sufficient importance to justify the shooting of any one, and this singular delusion was shared in by a large portion of the community.

"It is only a sectional contest," they said, but it is more than that for it involves the integrity of the United States and is therefore national and not sectional. The success of the South would mean separation, division, destruction; two hostile nations, with conflicting interests, two separate flags and two weak republics. I felt, therefore, that I was doing my duty; that was some consolation but I was already dreadfully homesick for all that, and an oppressive sense of loneliness crept over me. There was not a soul on the boat with whom I was acquainted and probably not one in the fort that I knew. All of my comrades seemed to be strangers to each other and stood silently leaning over the guard rail or sat motionless around the deck apparently buried in thought.

In passing 55th Street I strained my eyes in the direction of my sister's residence on First Avenue, but was only able to catch a glimpse of it and then the boat passed behind the stony walls of the prison on Blackwell's Island which effectually concealed it from my view. One by one we passed the little islands in the river and just before dark we reached the dock at Throgs Neck just below the Fort, which I was glad to learn was only sixteen or seventeen miles above New York City.

Abram Duryée (left) in the gray full-dress uniform of the 7th New York State Militia. [Patrick A. Schroeder Collection] Colonel Abram Duryée (right), 5th New York Infantry, 1861. [Brian C. Pohanka Collection]

CHAPTER 5.

*In which I arrive at Fort Schuyler and get a
taste of garrison life.*

Fort Schuyler is a large work of stone masonry, almost square in shape and pierced for two tiers of guns. It has an outside bastion of earth, faced with stone, to repel a land force, apparently stronger than the fort itself. It is situated on the extreme end of a point of land which projects out into the East River and completely commands the entrance to New York Harbor from the Sound. It was quite cold and the wind was blowing sharply when we landed upon the wharf. Five or six minutes of brisk marching brought us to a rough looking fence at the foot of a gently sloping hill which we ascended to the fort. The fence stretched completely across the narrowest part of the little peninsula and was guarded by four armed sentries. This was the limit of the enclosure in which the boys were allowed to ramble and they used to go down every day in crowds to see the visitors or purchase little articles of luxury from enterprising citizens who came up in wagons with pies and other delicacies, cigars and beer.

The first time I was placed on guard I was stationed on the outside of this fence, and in the evening the officer of the guard, Capt. Waugh of Company D made this impressive speech, "We have reason to believe there is a vessel trying to get out of New York Harbor with arms and ammunition for the rebels and it is necessary to be vigilant on your posts and keep a sharp lookout on the river for suspicious craft. The sentry who first discovers the vessel and gives the alarm will receive the thanks of the regiment and one thousand dollars in cash, but woe! woe!! woe!!! to the man I catch asleep at his post." I had never seen a suspicious craft, except in a novel, and didn't know exactly how to detect one. It might be a steamer or a canal boat and the uncertainty surrounding it made my duty as clear as Virginia mud. There were vessels of every description passing up and down the river but I didn't fire into any of them for two very excellent reasons. In the first place, I had no orders to do so and in the next place my musket was not loaded and unloaded muskets never go off except when some small boy aims one at his little sister.

I was in the best possible position to secure the reward for I was farthest from the fort and nearest to the water, but the night was as dark as pitch and I could see nothing a few yards beyond my nose, which felt like an icicle. For two long hours I stood shivering upon the beach earnestly watching for some mysterious vessel which would suddenly appear like a phantom ship, in a brilliant glare of blue flame and then suddenly vanish. After I had been on duty about two hours, when I turned my aching eyes from the river, they rested suddenly upon a dark suspicious looking object. After a moment's hesitation I moved boldly, but cautiously toward it. It proved to be a hungry dog in search of a bone. A few minutes later the relief guard came and I returned back to quarters.

The enclosed space appeared to be plenty large enough at first, but after a few days confinement it seemed to get tormentingly small. It was associated with tedious drills and tiresome parades. The little black saucy looking gunboat Vixen, anchored a little below the fort, overhauled a number of vessels and fired a shot across the bow of one that was endeavoring to pass without examination. The Vixen stopped everything that approached and permitted nothing to pass without a rigid examination. Our officer of the day became infected with the examining mania, and when going on guard later, I was peremptorily ordered to allow no one to leave without a written pass. I had just received this order when a young man named Tiebout, a member of the same company as myself, approached on a brisk trot. He had procured a pass and was endeavoring to reach the dock in time for the little steamer which was blowing her whistle ready to start. He had a resolute look which seemed to say "I am not to be trifled with." To stop a man in a hurry was an outrage. He denied my authority and refused to show his pass. He called me an insolent cub and said he was going to pass in spite of the opposition of a little runt like me. At the word runt my blood was up and when he attempted to pass, my bayonet was down at his breast in an instant. I was placed there to do what I was told to do and I was going to do it. The French soldier that ran Napoleon Bonaparte into the guardhouse for being without the countersign, and the Charge of the Light Brigade illustrated this idea. The order might be unreasonable, it might involve serious consequences, but when told to do a thing it was not to be questioned.

> "It was theirs not to make reply,
> Theirs not to reason why,
> Theirs but to do and die."

The promptness of my action appeared to be entirely unexpected and he recoiled a step from the point of the bayonet. The runt was suddenly transformed into a tiger and Tiebout finally submitted and was allowed to proceed. I am glad to know that my brave comrade never harbored any resentment against me for detaining him on this occasion. Tiebout became a brave and hardy soldier, one who was always reliable on the march and conspicuous in the field. I have seen him covered with dust and mud and blackened with powder, toiling over the bloody ground.

Sometime later we received our caps and the stovepipe hat being no longer needed was kicked out of shape by the men and landed in a trench.

When it came to selecting our company, I asked a companion, which he intended to join and he replied "Company F," for he was told they were a bully lot of boys and he was acquainted with the first lieutenant, Absalom Wetmore, who was a fine fellow. Four of us resolved to follow him. Company F was quartered in a long room and contained two fireplaces with cast iron mantles ornamented with two crossed cannons. The few men in the room informed us that they were on police duty while the company was drilling outside. They have charge of the quarters, sweep, scour kettles and pots and remove the rubbish outside the fort.

After a little while the company entered the room. Capt. Swartwout of Company F was a fine, gentlemanly looking man about thirty-five years old. He was of medium height with light chestnut hair, gray or blue eyes and quite prepossessing in appearance. He wore a mustache and whiskers which gave a military look to his handsome face in which there was an expression of quiet dignity which commanded respect. He talked very little but what he did say was pleasant and agreeable. When he dismissed the company they set up a deafening shout of joy and began dancing, singing, whistling, sparring and wrestling, making a Babel-like noise, generally. The men on police duty made a long table of boards and benches and each man took down a tin cup and plate from the mantel and waited for the order to "Fall in for supper," singing in the meantime, "A certain butcher had a dog and Bingo was his name." This song was introduced by Julius Cogswell, who afterwards was often called Bingo. Keeping time to the music, if such it could be called, the tin cups and plates were banged upon the table. Supper consisted of a thick slice of dry bread and about a pint of lukewarm tea. The table being full, I was obliged to eat on the floor. Hunger, however, easily adapts itself to circumstances. In less than five minutes after the slowest eater had risen from the table nearly every man was smoking. My own little briarwood was brought out and I diligently puffed away along with the rest. Later when the room had become quite dark I wrapped myself up in a blanket as others were doing and sauntered around the fort. I saw quite a number of large pieces of ordnance and mounted one to see the touch hole. It was on the top of this cannon that I first conceived the idea of keeping a journal and this work is the result. It was necessarily brief and imperfect and I am now, many years after the war, endeavoring to fill up the blanks from memory. I ascended a spiral stairway to the top of the fort and stood by the flagstaff for some time looking out over the water till the cold night air began to penetrate through my blanket, so I descended again. I visited Company A, attracted by the sound of a violin and was pleased with the quiet sociability of the men. When I returned to our quarters the men had spread the mattresses on the floor and shortly after drum beat we lay down side by side to joke and laugh ourselves to sleep.

CHAPTER 6.

*In which I introduce the reader to several of
my new acquaintances and we finally prepare
to leave the Fort.*

After breakfast we performed our toilets at the Fort
pump after which Ensign Carlyle Boyd took us out to drill.
Boyd had light hair and whiskers. His fingers were continually twisting his mustache, which the men dearly loved
to imitate. In the ranks behind his back, they mimicked
him and the whole drill was sometimes changed into bur-
lesque pantomime. Two of his most persistent tormentors
were Sullivan and Cogswell.

Sullivan was a noisy, turbulent and blustering little bully.
He was short, stout, strong, active and formidable with a
very quarrelsome disposition. Rough and rude in speech,
but plucky as a game rooster and ready to fight with any-
body, and the peacefully disposed avoided him. From the
very first there was something in his looks and behavior
toward me that caused me to regret that I hadn't really
studied "How to Box." I dreaded an encounter with such
a formidable antagonist, but thought it would be necessary
for one of us to whip the other in order to become friends.
Three or four days after I arrived at the Fort, Captain
Swartwout sized the men and placed me at the extreme left
of the line. Sullivan had been accustomed to take this place
and didn't seem to relish the change. He submitted un-
graciously, but the next time we fell in for drill Sullivan
and I fell out. He was already in line when I placed myself
in position on the outside and without saying a word he
promptly left his place and passed around to the left, leaving
a gap in the line which he expected me to close up. Without a moment's hesitation I passed around him in the same
manner, leaving a wider space and then he went around
me and in this childish manner we were getting farther and
farther from the company. The captain, glancing down
the line, ordered us to "Dress up on the left." In obedience
to the command I promptly placed myself on the left and
Sullivan coming up afterward, smilingly resumed his place

at the tail end with a triumphant shrug of his shoulders which exasperated me beyond endurance. I tried to get him to move up, which he refused to do, and suddenly grasping him by the coat collar I hurled him reeling, nearly into the arms of the captain. The captain, in a voice of thunder, angrily demanded why I did it. I explained as well as I could in a few words to the satisfaction of the captain who ordered Sullivan to resume his proper place. Sullivan was perfectly furious and grumbled and growled in an undertone throughout the entire drill, which to me seemed to be the low muttering sound of a coming storm, which would descend presently in a shower of blows. When we broke ranks, I waited quietly for the attack, but some miraculous reflection had disarmed his resentment. He never even mentioned the affair and what was still more wonderful, he treated me with more respect thereafter, and ultimately we became the very best of friends. Away down in the depths of Sullivan's turbulent nature there was a current of affectionate kindness, a little bubbling fountain of tenderness, unperceived except by those for whom he expressed a regard. I have occupied the same tent, drank from the same cup, and slept under the same blanket and underneath the roughness of the surface I found all the tenderness of a woman.

Julius Cogswell was a mixture of fox and monkey, not in appearance but by nature. He possessed all the cunning qualities of the one and all the mischievous propensities of the other. He would throw his mattress at somebody in the dark and be content to sleep on the floor without it, and his rations in the morning would follow his mattress, freely parting with a portion of his meal for the sake of hitting someone in the eye with a well-soaked crust or a piece of mealy potato. He was not vicious, just frolicksome.

We had a drill in the afternoon and a parade in the evening and this continued from day to day for nearly a month. The Confederates, meanwhile, were making things extremely lively and we were afraid the war would be over before we could reach the field. There had been no actual fighting except in the neighborhood of Charleston Harbor. The Confederate government had appointed a commission to Washington and they were endeavoring to create a feeling against the employment of force which was making itself felt throughout the land and a peaceful settlement was so confidently expected that we thought our military excursion to the southern states would prove a fiasco.

The parades in Fort Schuyler were formed by Adjutant Joseph E. Hamblin, a tall, well proportioned, genteel looking man with a bold, fearless face which seemed to me, a perfect model of manly beauty. There was an honest frankness, a rosy freshness, a genial cheerfulness that went direct to the heart and gave the impression that there was nothing narrow, mean or small, in the composition of its owner. There was an easy air of graceful dignity blended with good nature and sociability. In bodily formation this man, chisled in marble, would have rivaled the Apollo Belvedere. He was one of nature's masterpieces and the finest I ever saw. By his many engaging qualities he won the affection of the men; they loved, honored, almost idolized him. Later on, in gallant action, he was wounded at Cedar Creek and subsequently became a major-general.

In regimental popularity, Captain Hugh Judson Kilpatrick, of Company H, stood next to Adjutant Hamblin. Directly opposite in personal appearance he was a pony but not a runt. The little fellow was every inch a man, and the man was every inch a soldier. Boldness, fearlessness, activity, firmness and confidence were stamped so plainly in his countenance that everybody predicted a successful military career and they were right. He rose rapidly from a Captain of Infantry to a Colonel of Horse, from Colonel to Brigadier-General, and from Brigadier to Major-General of Cavalry.

He loved excitement and adventure and the whole Confederacy was none too big for him. He not only hunted for "Greybacks" in the jungles of the Chickahominy and in the suburbs of Richmond but chased the lions Hampton and Wheeler through the pines of Georgia and the palmettoes of Carolina. Two other regimental officers, Winslow and Davies, attracted my attention in Fort Schuyler. Davies was a little, stout, dark-complexioned man quite elegant looking but there was no external evidence of inward greatness, no outward mark of military genius, yet he became a Brigadier-General. Captain Cleaveland Winslow was a Frenchified-looking man with light hair and mustache carefully curled up like butchers' hooks. He was rather showy in dress. Instead of a military frock coat which was part of the uniform worn by the other officers, he wore a fancy Zouave jacket gaudily decorated. His military cap he jauntily wore on one side of the head. Altogether, he was half Italian bandit and half English highwayman, a romantic-looking fellow.

On the ninth of May, 1861, the regiment which had then become the Fifth New York State Volunteers was regularly sworn into the service of the United States and on Wednesday, the twenty-second, of the same month we struck our tents which we had occupied outside the fort and prepared to start. Just before we were accepted by the United States we were ordered to strip for a rigid medical examination and many of the men were rejected as physically unfit for the service. There were bodies and arms of every description, and if some of the legs could have been unscrewed and changed around it might have made an improvement. There was one poor little fellow with thin legs and arms, shivering with cold and shrinking with fear of being cast out, but he had the requisite number of toes and the constitution of a Shetland pony and was allowed to remain. If he had been rejected this history would never have been written.

CHAPTER 7.

In which we break up housekeeping in Fort
Schuyler and start for the war.

Man is a discontented animal, sometimes extremely hard
to please. He lives retrospectively and prospectively, always looking ahead or behind and his useless regrets for
the past and bright anticipations of the future cause him
to neglect the present. He looks back over the follies of
his past life and says with a sigh, "Ah! those were the good
old times," or looks forward saying, "There is a good time
coming." He doesn't appreciate the only time he has. If
we could properly appreciate our present enjoyments, forget the yesterdays, and "take no thought for the morrow,"
we would be much happier. As a proof of this we hailed
the order to "Strike tents" with shouts of joy and yet before
we had been many days in the wilderness of war we
"sighed for the fleshpots of Egypt," for the dirty cooks of
Fort Schuyler and the confinement of the garrison, as far
preferable to the privations of the field.

We had previously received our uniforms of red, white
and blue. Everybody wore these colors but we were covered all over with them. A more picturesquely unique and
fantastical costume could scarcely be conceived. The
breeches were wide flowing Zouave pants of a bright red,
narrow and pleated at the top, wide at the bottom and
baggy in the rear. These were topped with a broad sash
of the same color edged with blue tape and falling nearly
to the knee on the left side. The jacket was of coarse blue
material, trimmed with red tape, short, loose, low-necked
and collarless and rounded in front. The shirts were of the
same material with a broad stripe of red down the bosom.
The leggings were heavy white canvas, buttoned at the
side and reaching to the knee, and the shoes were clumsy,
square-toed scows. The caps were close-fitting red fezzes
turned back from the top of the head, to which was attached
a cord with a blue tassel that dangled down in the middle
of the back. These peakless caps afforded no protection
to our faces from the scorching rays of the hot sun and

we were bronzed like savages before we left the fort. After striking our tents, we waited patiently hour after hour for the boats to come and take us away but none appeared so we made huge fires out of the old flooring of our tents and passed the night upon the ground.

Cheerful parties gathered around the blazing boards and singing was the order of the evening. A man named Carrol of Company E sang "My Beautiful Muff" and "The Wake of Teddy Roe," and a man named Matthews of Company A sang the pathetic story of "The Ship That Went Down With the Fair Young Bride in the Waters of Dublin Bay." Poor Matthews was killed in the battle of Gaines' Mill, and Carrol was wounded and taken prisoner at the Second Battle of Bull Run. Sullivan entertained us with a patriotic song; he fancied he could sing but invariably pitched his music so high that his frantic efforts to get up where he wanted to go sounded like a parrot imitating a steam whistle. The men would call out to him "Come down, Sullivan, come down."

In the morning we found the boats fastened to the wharf and by noon we embarked. The banks of the river were lined with people who cheered and waved handkerchiefs as we passed them on our way. At Astoria, where I had formerly resided, a little brass cannon was set off as a salute to which we replied with hearty cheers. Even the poor prisoners on Blackwell's Island in their ring-streaked uniforms, temporarily forgot their shame in a burst of patriotism. As we neared the dock at the foot of Twenty-third Street we could see that it was black with human beings and we could scarcely wedge our way through, after landing. They were the relatives and friends of the sun-burned heroes from Throg's Neck and had assembled with throbbing hearts and tearful faces to say once more the most difficult thing in the English language, "Good-bye, Tom," "Good-bye, Billy, God bless you." Many aged fathers and mothers on that dock saw for the last time their beloved sons, who were soon to sleep in unknown graves, beneath the green fields that were ploughed up with shot and enriched with the blood of both sections. Many would meet no more until they "met beyond the river" where man does not grapple with his fellow man in deadly conflict, and where peace reigns forever. Comparatively few of my gallant comrades returned as I did to share the benefits of a lasting peace and many who did were disfigured with scars or crippled for life.

There was very little time for farewells for we were obliged to hurriedly push our way through in single file, and no one could stop a moment without detaining all the rest. One anxious look, one hurried word, a pressure of the hand, and we were gone. No relative or friend of mine was there to meet me, there having been a misunderstanding about the time of our arrival, and while my friends were waiting for more definite information I was marching through the city.

After forcing a passage through the crowd, the battalion was formed in marching order on First Avenue and we started toward Third Avenue closely followed by a sidewalk committee of friends and relatives. How firmly and proudly we marched through our native city, carefully keeping step to the music of the band. Fathers and mothers held their little ones high in their arms above the heads of the multitude, trying to impress upon their tender minds the fact that we were going to fight, and die if necessary, for the pretty little flags they waved with childish glee. We marched through Twenty-third Street to Third Avenue, down Third Avenue to Fourteenth Street, across Fourteenth to Broadway, and down Broadway to City Hall Park where we were reviewed by the great Tycoon, Fernando Wood, the Mayor of Gotham. After the review we retraced our steps through Broadway to Canal Street and down to the river, where we embarked on board the steamer Alabama for Fortress Monroe. The vessel was small and the men were huddled together like cattle in a pen. The next day we passed the steamer Cambridge on her way from Dixie and the two vessels fired a salute. The following day, May 26, we came in sight of Fortress Monroe after a delightful sail.

CHAPTER 8.

Our arrival in Virginia.

Fortress Monroe, largest and strongest fort in the United States, is situated on a little island in Chesapeake Bay, at the entrance to Hampton Roads, the outlet of the James, Elizabeth and Nansemond rivers, and completely covers the approach to these rivers from the bay. Between the James and York rivers lies a tract of land called the Peninsula, every foot of which possesses deep historic interest. About midway between Fortress Monroe and the opposite shore at the mouth of Hampton Roads is an artificial island of rocks called the Rip Raps made by the government to assist the fort in its defensive work.

Two or three vessels of war were anchored off the fort when we landed and as we approached the crews climbed into the rigging and gave us cheer after cheer. About two o'clock we landed at a wharf below the fort and took up a line of march along a dusty road, crossing a long rickety bridge over a shallow stream, halting in a field near the home of Joseph Segar, fronting the entrance of Hampton Roads. The first unmistakable evidence that we were in Dixie Land came curling upward over the tree tops, at first a light wreath and afterward a huge volume of dense black smoke. Some of the men climbed into the trees and reported a town on fire. The people of Hampton were preparing to leave and they were burning the bridge to prevent pursuit.

As the shades of evening approached and no wagons appeared, it became evident that we were going to have neither tents nor ammunition and we accordingly prepared to bivouac on the field. The last night in Fort Schuyler was passed beneath the broad canopy of heaven, unsheltered from the falling dew, and the first night in the "Old Dominion" would be spent beneath the same "overhanging firmament," the same "majestical roof fretted with golden fire" and dripping with moisture from a southern sky. The hot sun went slowly down in the west, and a cool breeze springing up, the men without waiting for orders collected rails from the fences and kindled fires to boil their coffee.

Afterward the boys spread their ponchos on the ground and the whole regiment, tired and exhausted, was soon fast asleep, dreaming, perhaps, of home and friends that some would never see again. I was terribly annoyed at first by insects, but falling asleep, was not troubled with dreams and I arose at the sound of the drum, refreshed and invigorated with my first night's repose on the bosom of the "mother of presidents."

The next day, Sunday, I rambled off across the fields to the beach beyond Segar's mansion and along the sandy shore. The houses I passed were all deserted, not a sound was heard and I felt sick at heart and deplored the horrors of war. God grant that the owners may be able to return to their homes. During the day the tents arrived and were put up, ammunition was served out and camp was established.

CHAPTER 9.

Camp Hamilton.

On Monday, May 27, 1861, we were prohibited from going in the direction of the old bridge leading to the fort, but were allowed to ramble off into the orchard near by and lie down in the heat of the day under the refreshing shade of the fruit trees, or wander away across the field beyond to bathe in the waters of Hampton Roads. Many a time have I reclined near this beautiful bay and gazed out over the rippling waters, sparkling and flashing in the sunlight, until I have been lulled to sleep by the soft and musical murmur of the wavelets as they dashed playfully over the beach.

Away to the right was a thickly wooded strip of land ending in a point called Newport News, fortified by United States troops under the command of General Phelps. Off to the left of Newport News was the mouth of the Nansemond River and near it the powerful Confederate battery at Pig Point.

Colonel Duryee, before we left the Alabama, is said to have promised to lead us against the battery on Sewall's Point in the course of a day or two and I wondered why he wasn't making some preparation to fulfill his promise, and already in my imagination we were mounting the breastworks as they do in novels and scattering haughty Southerners like sheep. I'd be a hero, of course, if there were any Confederate flags to tear down or great generals to rescue. I'd be just the boy to do it.

Since our arrival at camp we had heard very little from the direction of Hampton and I was burning with impatience to look at the village and the burnt bridge, and the order not being strict, the sentries did not try to keep us in "close confinement," so early the next day I slipped out unobserved and started off toward Hampton. The bridge was an ordinary wooden structure, only about half destroyed. The village on the opposite side of the stream was without exception the most beautiful town I had ever beheld. Large, fine-looking houses and neat cottages all painted white, with white fences and green shade trees, gave the place an air of neatness and cleanliness, and I could almost fancy that I could smell the fragrance of the flowers that were blooming around these dwellings. I hailed a negro to convey me across and was soon landed on the other side.

I stopped to speak to two or three darkies in the village, who informed me that the place was not deserted by the inhabitants until our regiment made its appearance at Old Point. "Dey didn't care for dem yoder sojers, but when dey seen you red-legged debbils comin' right past, dey grab up eberything dey kin and run like the old boy was arter 'em." How many white people remained in the village I do not know, but there were some, for a few days afterward I went with members of the Troy regiment to the house of a man named Jones, in search of his brother, a rank Secessionist, and for some time a spy for the "Trojan camp." A reward had been offered for the head of this man and the rumor was that the head was valued at two hundred dollars. The Troy soldiers were very anxious to secure it. An old lady about sixty, and unmistakably white, opened the door and we inquired for Colonel Jones. "Yes, he is in," she said and just then the gentleman himself appeared. "Come in, gentlemen, come in," said he composedly. "The weather is warm outside, the sun is hot, and you look jaded. It's not often that we receive visitors in these days, but you are welcome." We smoked and talked for about an hour, passing the time quite pleasantly, and when we arose to depart we had never once mentioned the object of our visit.

CHAPTER 10.

Picket Duty.

The first time I went on picket duty I was placed on Post Number 14. The post ran along the edge of a marsh. About eleven o'clock I heard the sentry on Post Number 12 excitedly challenging somebody in the swamp, and after the third command the loud report of a musket immediately followed the sentry's call, which was rapidly repeated from post to post. A Frenchman belonging to one of the other companies was acting corporal, and after floundering around in the mud finally succeeded in starting up something in the bushes and pursued it through the briars behind Post Number 13 toward the place where I was stationed, shouting, "Stop him, stop him, stop him!" I hurried to the opening on my post and just as I reached it I heard a terrific snort and the sharp report of a rifle, and while feeling around my leg to find out where I was wounded, something darted past me and scampered across the fields. Suddenly the Frenchman with his murderous gun appeared in the opening wildly inquiring "Vere is he?" "Where is what?" I answered. "Ze man, ze rebel!" "That wasn't a man," I said coolly, "it was a pig." He was terribly disappointed in not capturing his first rebel and sullenly walked back to camp.

On another occasion I was detailed for picket duty on the shore of Hampton Roads with three others at the Seminary, a large brick building five or six stories high, bearing an oblong tablet with the inscription "Female College," from which all had fled except Professor Raymond and family. We were ordered to be vigilant and given to understand that it was a very dangerous position. The officer in charge was Sergeant Sovereign. The sergeant was to relieve the men at regular intervals and under no circumstances to absent himself from the post until relieved. As the evening approached, the promised supper did not appear. Could it be possible we had been forgotten? John Brown requested that he be allowed to make a short cut through the swamp and bring back something to eat but was denied permission. Professor Raymond with true Southern hospitality invited us to his table. Brown asked, "If that's the way old Virginia treats invaders, what does she do with her distinguished guests?" "Hangs them," said the Sergeant dryly, "when she finds their name is Brown."

The next morning I was sent to report to the officer of the day. The colonel to whom I was conducted manifested considerable indignation for our being so grossly neglected. "Forty-eight hours on duty without food" was entered in the orders of the day and our names were conspicuously mentioned as "entitled to all praise."

The next day Captain Kilpatrick was to take a portion of his company out on a scouting expedition. I was wild to go and boldly asked permission. "What company do you belong to?" "Company F." "Does your Captain know of this request?" "No, sir." "What is your name?" "Thomas P. Southwick." "Were you one of the men stationed at the Seminary?" "Yes, sir." "Well, if you can obtain your Captain's consent I haven't the least objection." Captain Swartwout listened attentively but declined to grant permission, saying, "If anything happens to my men I want to be with them. In a few days I intend to take Company F out and you shall certainly go with me. You mustn't be disappointed, Southwick," said he kindly as I turned away, "we'll have plenty to do yet and I'll not forget you."

Preparations for a great battle were being made in and around Washington where a large army, mostly uniformed militia, was being formed under Major General McDowell, and in the neighborhood of Harpers Ferry under General Patterson, and at Fortress Monroe under General Butler.

On the evening of the twenty-third of May, 1861, several surprise parties were formed in the National Capital and early on the twenty-fourth, men could be seen crossing the long bridge over the Potomac, and others fantastically dressed embarked upon steamers and sailed down the river to Alexandria. A large number of the inhabitants had left the town but some who ought to have gone remained, one of these a saloon-keeper named Jackson. Jackson had placed over his house what most of the visitors considered an objectionable flag and was quietly reposing under it. Early in the morning there was a sound of musketry in the neighborhood of this house and the flag disappeared. Later, two men were lying dead within a few feet of each other, Elmer Ellsworth and Jackson.

A company of the 5th New York drills in Scott's Tactics at Camp Hamilton, circa July 1861. [Brian C. Pohanka Collection]

CHAPTER 11.

Battle of Big Bethel.

June ten, 1861.—The men were quietly sleeping beneath their white tents and all was still around the camp. About the hour of midnight the order suddenly came "Fall in, in light marching order, with one day's rations." Stealthily the sergeants called the men, warning them not to make any noise, and silently like spectres they poured out in the darkness, so dense that we could scarcely recognize the comrade by our side. Each man was ordered to bind the white scarf of his turban around his left arm to distinguish each other in the dark. We emerged silently and took our places in line. "Right face; forward, march" was given in an undertone and off we started across the field and joined the Second and Tenth New York Regiments.

When we reached the burnt bridge on the banks of Hampton Creek, we awaited transportation, and bye and bye several monster scows glided toward us, propelled by oars muffled in their locks, and conveyed us across. The village of Hampton was as quiet as a graveyard. We marched over the ground beyond the village as fast as darkness would permit, when we suddenly came across some other soldiers resting by the roadside. They had come over some other road and waited for us to pass, which we did in perfect silence, the same way we had passed other companies along the line. We had now quite a respectable little army.

We were proceeding along at a lively gait and had just entered a wood when a volley of musketry suddenly rang out, bringing the whole regiment up with a jerk. Fortunately the pieces were aimed too high and no one was struck. At the sound we all came to a full stop and every man's musket came down from the shoulder, and "click, click, click" went the locks along the whole line. It was a strange sound in the stillness of the wood and terribly exciting, although no word was spoken. Eight hundred fingers rested upon eight hundred triggers and twice eight hundred eyes tried to penetrate the darkness of the impenetrable wood. Then came a whisper along the line that we had driven in the rebel pickets. In a few minutes the colonel shouted "Attention, battalion!" and "Forward, march!" and we were once more advancing, some beginning to sing in an undertone "A certain butcher had a dog and Bingo was his name," but before the chorus was reached it was suppressed.

In the morning we heard a terrific fire of musketry some distance away. The enemy was in our rear and we were two miles ahead of the nearest of our troops. We soon learned the history of a most unfortunate mistake. Two regiments marching along different roads suddenly came upon each other in the dark and each mistaking the other for the enemy, opened fire. All chances of surprising the enemy were now gone. Colonel Duryee was the first to leave a group of officers in consultation, and stepping briskly into the middle of the road ordered the men "Right about face! Forward, march!" and once more we were headed in the direction of the enemy. In passing a house later, an old man standing in a doorway deliberately fired a bullet into the ranks of a Vermont regiment, wounding one of the Green Mountain boys in the thigh.

We were conducted away from the road to the edge of a ploughed field. "Now, boys," said Colonel Duryee, pointing calmly across the field, "the enemy is over in that wood. I want every man to do his duty. The eyes of the whole country are upon you. Fire low and be careful of your ammunition." Then in a loud voice he gave the order to charge. With a shout the regiment started across the ploughed field and soon the muskets began to snap and crack and bullets began to whistle around us pretty lively. The regiment was formed in line of battle facing the enemy and advanced for some distance through the wood, but the bullets rained down upon us so thickly and the artillery fire became so heavy that we were compelled to seek the shelter of the trees. The fire of the enemy was so heavy and incessant that it was impossible to reform our ranks. Everybody seemed to be fighting on his own hook. In the midst of the wood, stretched out stiff and stark in death, was a member of our regiment. Over him someone had laid a blanket. I lifted the blanket but failed to recognize him, but read the white strap of his canteen, "Tibout, Company A." Off on the dusty road lay the mangled body of an officer in the uniform of the regular army. It was the lifeless body of Major Theodore Winthrop, a gallant soldier from Massachusetts who had gone from the scene of strife with the humble Zouave private to the land of eternal rest.

I was granted permission to crawl up further in the wood to see the enemy's battery. I was stopped pretty soon by Captain Davies, who demanded where I was going and that I come back or he'd blow my infernal head off. After explaining, he permitted me to proceed. On my hands and knees I went, drawing my musket after me. Presently I came to a field of growing corn, too high to see over. I tried here and there to peep through the corn and was just turning away when I perceived the chaplain of our regiment, Captain Winslow's father, standing near the fence with a big cavalry pistol in his hand. I left him there and returned to the company. Nearly three years afterward this old gentleman, while returning with the dead body of his son, fell overboard and was drowned in the Potomac River.

For hours the enemy had persistently endeavored to shell us out of the wood. For hours the Union artillery had gallantly maintained its position. For hours men had been firing from behind trees and bushes, and the sun was descending and the shades of evening settling around the wounded and dead. The men were tired, hungry, sick and disheartened, blackened with powder and covered with dirt, but there were no laurel wreaths of fame around their brows. Our regiment must have been the last to leave, for we could see no other troops behind us and we lagged along wearily, dragging our footsteps over the dusty ground, almost ready to drop. A man named Murphy and myself on reaching Hampton entered one of the deserted houses and slept till morning.

CHAPTER 12.

The First Battle of Bull Run.

Immediately after the battle of Big Bethel our regiment settled down to the conviction that the war was going to last for some time. The days passed slowly and tediously at Camp Hamilton. Joe Segar's orchard was my favorite resort in dry weather and when not drilling or engaged in any other duty I'd lie under the apple trees reading my constant companion, Shakespeare, which I always carried with me.

On July fifth, 1861, President Lincoln called for four hundred thousand men and four hundred million dollars to put down the rebellion.

On July twenty-one, 1861, the first great battle of the war was fought, between General McDowell and Confederate Generals Beauregard and Johnston at Bull Run. A large body of armed men was placed on the bank of the Bull Run stream. A military excursion from Washington would have to pass and everybody anticipated striking results from the advance of these peacemakers across the country. They endeavored to cross but were violently assailed. For several hours the rattle of musketry was incessant along the pretty stream. There was a stone bridge on the Warrenton Pike over Bull Run and the head of McDowell's forces marched in a direct line from the village toward this bridge, while a body about sixteen or seventeen thousand strong went on a roundabout route to Sudley's Ford in order to attack the enemy's left flank. In order to reach Richmond the enemy had to be dislodged from his position along the stream. The enemy strengthened his position on the right. General McDowell suddenly attacked him on the left, but owing to the soldierly instinct of Confederate General Barnard E. Bee coming to the rescue a decisive victory for McDowell was frustrated. The Second Rhode Island Regiment, with colors flying, boldly advanced in the open field beyond the stone bridge, having crossed Bull Run at Sudley's Ford, and gallantly charged the open space to drive the South Carolinians from a thicket where they lay concealed. The South Carolinians were supported by the whole battalion of Louisiana Tigers with two six-pound howitzers. The brave Rhode Island boys with shattered lines were compelled to fall back without accomplishing their object.

Again with Burnside's whole brigade they advanced to the attack, over the bloody ground, but were obliged to withdraw to the shelter of the woods. Before the third and final charge was made Generals Bee and Bartow had reinforced the stubborn Carolinians, and the Union troops also were strengthened with Heintzelman's Division on the right and Tyler's Division, which had boldly waded through Bull Run stream, on the left. The brave Carolinians were driven from their shelter as the excursionists advanced and the fierce Tigers of Louisiana were driven through the jungles, while Bee and Bartow were hurled back some distance and finally retreated in confusion.

Up to this time everything was favorable to the Union army. The McDowellites were jubilant. Stealing up the sloping side of a plateau, in the face of heavy artillery fire, the victorious troops advanced and soon the whole of the elevated position was in their possession.

In a house on the hill lay a sick lady, emaciated, unable to move, who shudderingly listened to the sound of the approaching conflict, till the bursting shells and solid shot came crashing through the house. Beyond this house the enemy was re-forming and massing and a terrific conflict commenced for the recovery of the plateau. Five batteries of guns were employed and about eight or ten thousand men were hurled with resistless force against the Union forces who were gallantly trying to retain their position and were finally driven from the hill. Again and again they advanced, the place was taken and retaken until after a severe and protracted struggle the Union troops were pressed down the murderous slope, leaving several guns in the hands of the enemy, who lost two generals. The sick woman was found dead with five or six frightful wounds on her body. The battle now broke fiercely out upon the right. Reinforcements were constantly arriving on the

Confederate side and the tired soldiers of McDowell were pressed back, fighting desperately as they retired, yielding only to the pressure of superior numbers, and thus the battle ended.

Immediately after the Battle of Bull Run, our regiment was ordered to hold itself in readiness to move, and a short time after we struck tents and moved from Camp Hamilton into Fortress Monroe. We moved after dark and embarked on a steamer for Washington, where it was supposed the Confederates were preparing to visit us. In going up Chesapeake Bay we passed the mouth of the Potomac River and proceeded around to Baltimore, where we made a camp on Federal Hill.

Shortly after the battle of Bull Run, General George B. McClellan was placed in command of the Army of the Potomac.

Non-Commissioned Staff Mess, Camp Hamilton, 1861. Adjutant Hamblin seated at left, and Sergeant Charles F. Mather, the 6'4½" former Color Bearer, at right. [Brian C. Pohanka Collection]

CHAPTER 13.

Federal Hill, Baltimore.

Many changes took place in the regiment during our stay in Baltimore. Colonel Abram Duryee was appointed on the staff of General Dix and shortly afterward became a Brigadier General, Lieutenant-Colonel Gouverneur R. Warren taking his place; Hiram Duryee, the great starch manufacturer was promoted from a subordinate position to Lieutenant-Colonelcy, and Captain Swartwout of our company resigned to accept a position in the artillery service. Lieutenant Oliver Whetmore assumed command but resigned on account of ill health, and Sergeant Wheeler was promoted to the vacancy.

Shortly after our occupation of Federal Hill, I found myself, with about fifty others, in the guardhouse. Having "run the guard," I was placed in "durance vile." We had a jolly time singing, shouting and amusing ourselves. The men procured candles, plastering them all over the walls, and when the other lights were extinguished the guardhouse burst forth with a grand illumination. The men danced around like the disciples of Zoroaster over the sacred fire, when suddenly there appeared in the doorway a dark object with a naked flashing sword and the next moment darkness reigned and the voice of the colonel alone was heard. The next morning he marched up and down in front of us, finally addressing us in a solemn and impressive manner. "There's not a man that shouldn't hang his head in shame." After a few more words of reproach and a touching appeal to our sense of honor and the credit of the regiment, he dismissed us magnanimously to our respective companies. That evening on parade I was appointed corporal. It was so totally unexpected that I scarcely realized the fact until my friends began to congratulate me, and then visions of greatness began to rise before me and I saw Napoleon, the little Corporal of France, in the humble title that had been bestowed upon me. It released me from manual labor; I was to be a "boss soldier." It placed a restraint upon my actions. The city with its attractions must be shut out, the girls I had run the guard to see would have to come to camp or secure some other chap, and the theatre would lose an occasional attendant. The last play that I saw was "The Life and Death of King Richard the Third," and John Wilkes Booth was the actor. That night I was out without leave and Colonel Warren occupied a conspicuous place where he could plainly see me in the audience.

For days there were rumors around the camp of some movement about to take place and my company was one of the number selected to go under heavy marching orders for an expedition to—no one seemed to know where.

The people of Baltimore turned out "en masse" to see us off, and we embarked on a steamer for some unknown destination. The next morning we were close in toward the eastern shore of Chesapeake Bay, feeling our way carefully along, advancing and backing off, making little progress. The tide was falling and we were falling off with the tide and eventually became stuck in the mud so effectually that it took two tugs to pull us off. At last we reached the mouth of the Pocomoke River, a picturesque stream, so narrow that the overhanging branches of the trees interlaced each other in some places. Eventually we reached a place called Snow Hill and here we found two or three thousand soldiers of the Delaware Legion awaiting our arrival to start on an expedition down the peninsula. The roads were sandy and the distance between towns sometimes considerable. We were on the road to Pungoteague, Virginia, wherever that might be, and finally pushed on to Drummondtown. After reaching the latter town we returned to Federal Hill and the whole expedition appeared like a farce.

Later the whole army was concentrated at Fortress Monroe. Our regiment was pushed forward and encamped some distance beyond the village of Hampton, which had been burned by the Confederates. Nothing was left standing but a wilderness of blackened chimneys.

The next day we moved forward toward Yorktown, passing the fortifications of Big Bethel, the extent of whose earthworks astonished us. We reached the rear of the army at nightfall and encamped near the brigade of General Sykes.

Saturday, April fifth, eighteen sixty-two. We were aroused at three o'clock this morning and everything being in readiness by seven, off we started. I had secured very little sleep for there was a terrific storm during the early part of the evening, and at twelve I was obliged to awaken the wood and water detail for the benefit of the cook. The roads were muddy and the marching very bad. We marched several miles nearer to Yorktown.

April eleven we broke camp in the morning and moved still nearer to Yorktown. A system of fortifications of the most formidable nature extended around Yorktown and the big, black guns were as thick as crows in an unprotected cornfield.

Zouaves go through the motions of McClellan's Bayonet Exercise at Federal Hill. [Illustration by Thur de Thulstrup]

CHAPTER 14.

Before Yorktown.

April thirteen, eighteen sixty-two. Seated on the snarp edge of two or three rails, I am endeavoring to write under trying circumstances. From where I sit I have an excellent view of the ground occupied by Fitz John Porter's division. Our camp, consisting of ponchos on stakes and pine boughs, presents a picturesque appearance. Innumerable camps like ours are stretched all over the country as far as the eye can reach.

The enemy force is variously estimated to be from twenty to one hundred and fifty thousand men, but I suppose they really number about fifteen thousand, for Magruder never had more than that number.

There is heavy firing from a big gun on the water as I write and report says it proceeds from the Merrimac. Early this morning a balloon was sent up, making observations. The balloon and telegraph wire are now extensively used in military operations. On our muddy march from Hampton to "Camp Misery" the telegraph followed us and the men employed in digging the holes and setting the poles proceeded nearly as fast as we marched. "Little Mac," as the men love to call McClellan, could receive and convey intelligence to Fortress Monroe without leaving his tent, which is a great improvement over the old plan, although beacon fires, signals, rockets and lights are still necessary.

April seventeen. I was convinced today that the enemy could build batteries and very decent ones, too. While constructing a military road of logs we came across an earthwork they had built which it seemed a pity to abandon.

All day long heavy rifled siege guns and pontoon boats were carried past us and the work went steadily on, indicating that Yorktown will certainly fall.

April eighteen, eighteen sixty-two. The troops on both sides are becoming bolder and more aggressive. Last night the camp was startled by the booming of a gun that fairly shook the earth and rumbled through the sky like a peal of thunder. "Just listen to the birdie sing," shouted the men.

April nineteen. The enemy made a sortie last night but was repulsed and driven back.

The New York Times of the Twenty-first says, "The Fifth Regiment of New York Volunteers is considered the best drilled regiment in the army before Yorktown. They have been appointed to a post of honor and are the only volunteers in the division of the regular soldiers of the United States Army."

Since we have been here the height of my ambition has been to see Yorktown, and I have endeavored in various ways to satisfy my curiosity. I have climbed trees like Zacchaeus and hills like Balboa but yesterday when I least expected it my efforts were crowned with success for I saw from the banks of the York River the hills of Yorktown and Gloucester with the Confederate flag of stars and bars floating over them.

April twenty-seven. Our company with two others was ordered out on picket. While standing in the rain waiting for further instructions I heard a captain tell Lieutenants Sovereign and Cartwright that the enemy made another sortie last night.

April twenty-eight. Our company and Company A received orders to pack up and we were soon on the road toward Ship Point. Owing to the muddy road we had to march in single file and the water in some places was actually knee deep. We saw several shipwrecked army wagons drawn by mules so stubborn and lazy that they preferred to lie down and roll in the mud instead of discharging their military duty.

Cheeseman's Landing is situated on a creek about three miles from Camp Winfield Scott near the mouth of the York River. The water being deep enough for the purpose, it was selected as a harbor for some of the magnificent floating hospitals, such as the Commodore and Wilson's Small, both handsome steamers fitted up for the reception of wounded soldiers. A dock was afterward constructed of old flatboats for the purpose of unloading the huge mortars and mortar beds or carriages to be used in the siege of Yorktown. Arms and ammunition are brought here and unloaded and sent forward to the works as fast as they can be finished by the soldiers, who work like beavers, throwing up batteries with their sinewy arms, regardless of both heat and rain.

The mail boat Nelly Baker arrives every day with welcome letters and newspapers. She brings pies, too, and bread and cakes. When we reached the landing where many boats were lying, we promptly relieved the First Connecticut troops who were unloading ammunition.

The time had now arrived for the reduction of Yorktown and the general assault would take place the following day. All night long, however, the enemy was quietly moving out of town before we could get a pop at them. There was nothing left to fight. Our company was on detail when the news arrived and we could hardly believe it.

May six. Rained like fury all night.

Bands are permitted to play once more and ours is now performing in the camp street.

On Friday, the ninth of May, our whole division started forward in the direction of the abandoned town. The road was dusty and the day suffocatingly hot. Wormly Creek runs along by the side of the road and how beautifully the glassy water of the placid stream reflects the trees and shrubbery. How the little birds go tripping from branch to branch as we march in solid column beneath. Hark to the sound of our heavy feet as we "tramp, tramp, tramp" over the sacred soil of Virginia, our tin cups clanging at every step against our plethoric haversacks and the straps of our heavy knapsacks straining and creaking on our aching shoulders. See the head of the column ascending the little hills in the distance, turning and twisting like a huge

52

serpent, the polished muskets glistening in the sun as the rays of "Old Sol" strike upon them. How gaily the men are singing. Listen! " 'Tis the Star-Spangled Banner, oh long may it wave." A thousand tongues are chanting the patriotic hymn. It swells upon the air and is wafted by the breeze over the hills of Yorktown, hallowed by the feet of Washington and Lafayette, a land wrested from British misrule by the patriotic devotion of a people determined to be free; heroes, who now slumber peacefully beneath the soil of their agitated country. Awake! Martyrs of the Revolution, Awake! Do you not hear that soul-stirring air? The heroes of today are marching over your graves, Heroes of the past. They are bearing that flag triumphantly over you. They are singing the song to the flag that you have bequeathed them, a flag that has been banished and a song that has not been sung over these hills for a year.

We saw the graves of the Confederate dead, a vast sloping field of little mounds, and judging by the number, the mortality must have been fearful. Little shapeless pieces of wood are stuck in the ground. I tread softly over these graves for the road runs through them and we walk over them, who are enemies no more. "They might have died in a better cause," I heard a captain say, "but who is competent to judge the cause for them? They had decided the matter for themselves and were true to their convictions even unto death."

A little to the right of the graveyard was a line of rifle pits and nearby a number of dirty and ragged tents. On the side of one, boldly inscribed in charcoal, were the words "Come along, Yank, there's room outside to bury you."

CHAPTER 15

On the march.

The road to Williamsburg was fairly covered with dead horses and the stench that proceeded from them was almost intolerable. It was a long march, this march of ours from Yorktown to Williamsburg, and nearly half of the regiment, before we reached our destination, fell exhausted by the wayside. I was weak from the effects of a cold, and the fierce sun beating upon my aching head seemed as if it would scorch up what little brains I had left.

The straps of my knapsack, which never seemed so heavy before, cut into my shoulders and into the cords of my neck, making it ache the more. We were in pursuit, however, actually following up the enemy, and that kept me up for some time, while my legs mechanically kept straight ahead as if they had been wound up and set in motion like a clock. The springs and pulleys, however, at last began to give way and I, who had hitherto considered myself a little Ajax in strength, was obliged at last to "cave in" and Murphy and I fell out of the ranks and lay down beneath a tree and slept until the provost guard aroused us and forced us along the dusty road.

About half a mile from Williamsburg we halted on the exact battlefield of the sixth, where Hooker and Hancock contended with Longstreet for four or five hours before they were allowed to proceed. There had evidently been a fight and a pretty severe one. The enemy fought stubbornly and our forces were three or four times driven back. The final charge of our troops was made under the supposition that we were receiving reinforcements and the impression was encouraged by the bands in the rear patriotically playing the national airs.

To show how near a defeat this battle of Williamsburg was, it is only necessary to read McClellan's lugubrious dispatch to the Secretary of War the next day in which he says, "My entire force is considerably inferior to that of the enemy, who will fight well, but I will do my best with the troops at my disposal." McClellan's fear of having too small a force was no doubt the cause of his seeming inactivity. The village of Williamsburg was a beautifully romantic, dreamy old town, the streets being regularly laid out, the houses neat and clean. In a field on the outskirts of the town a regiment of New Hampshire troops was encamped, and here again we stopped to rest, my companion this time being Stephenson, for I had outwalked Murphy and overtaken Stephenson, and we trudged the last two or three miles together, eluding the provost guard this time in the tall wheat. A good Samaritan, a native of the town, gave us a good cup of coffee. Pleading illness, Stephenson and I engaged the hospitality of the men from the Granite State and remained till nearly sundown before resuming our journey. On leaving we took the telegraph for a guide and tramped about three more miles beyond the village, and there being no prospect of reaching camp before morning we followed the example of others and slept in undisturbed tranquillity till daylight.

Reached camp about half-past seven and had barely time to cook our coffee before the brigade started forward again. Falling out became so fashionable that Captain Warren said he intended to reverse the order and ride behind the battalion and give his personal attention to cases of prostration. Naturally there wasn't a single case of the malady reported that day.

We stopped at Ropers Meeting House and remained there the following day. A few days later we were halting on a road when the major rode madly down the line ordering us in an excited tone to "Unsling knapsacks and fall in with haversacks and canteens." The enemy had driven in some of our cavalry and destroyed vast quantities of army stores, was the report. No one seemed to know how they appeared on the flank. Our knapsacks were left in the wood and off we started on a "double quick," passing a portion of General Franklin's division marching from West Point. The contents of our canteens being exhausted there was a loud and pressing demand for water. No one dared to leave the ranks to secure any except the drummers and they were offered as much as fifty cents for a canteen full. I thought of the well in the valley of Samaria and the fresh waters in the oasis of Saharia (Sahara). After tramping about a mile or so we were drawn in line of battle and ordered to "load." Bayonets were fixed and a company was rapidly deployed as skirmishers. There must have been some kind of a row that ended in a stampede, for troop after troop of cavalry in full retreat came dashing back. We were permitted after a while to stack arms, break ranks and procure water. We were momentarily expecting the order to advance, but evening settled without a Confederate appearing in view.

There is nothing in the world so refreshing to the soldier as a cup of coffee. I didn't have any and Sullivan very kindly insisted on sharing his with me, so I gathered some twigs and soon had the satisfaction of seeing the water simmer, when the colonel called the regiment to "attention." I managed to get some coffee into the water and with Sullivan's assistance contrived to get some of it, grounds and all, into my canteen. Anderson's Zouaves had come to relieve us and we marched back to the wood where we had left our knapsacks, a discouraged and dispirited body of men. There was an unnatural glare of light and we were filled with consternation to find the place on fire. Our knapsacks had been saved by the men of other regiments who dragged them aside to a place of safety.

The prompt action of the army on this occasion was caused by the Confederate general of cavalry, who boldly rode around the rear of the entire army, snapping up stragglers and taking horses calculated to be of service to the Confederacy. The sudden appearance of the enemy was a complete surprise. Some of our regiments had made a mistake and were proceeding steadily in the wrong direction. The Sixth Cavalry was in advance and jogging along when they were confronted by a large body of Confederate Cavalry and after a sharp engagement were driven back on the road. This caused the alarm, the stampede and the preparation in the wood to receive the triumphant foe.

We lost considerable time identifying our knapsacks and took a narrow path through the woods to regain the right road. The army in the meantime had advanced and was preparing to spend the night in its new position. It was still light and the road leading over the summit of a high hill overlooked the largest and most beautiful valley I ever beheld. It was covered with encampments and the ruddy glare of a thousand camp fires illuminated the scene.

Fifty or sixty thousand soldiers occupied this valley and their dark forms stood out conspicuously in the glorious light of the burning logs. It was a magnificent sight, a sight such as Balaam must have seen from the top of Mount Peor when he "lifted up his eyes and he saw Israel abiding in his tents" and enthusiastically exclaimed "How goodly are thy tents, O! Israel. As the valleys are they spread forth, as gardens by the river's side, as the trees of lign aloes which the Lord hath planted, and as cedar trees beside the waters."

On the right of the camp, shining like gold beneath the light of the camp fires, could be seen the calm waters of the crooked river and two or three small vessels were anchored in the stream near a little group of houses which constitutes the village of Cumberland. Here in this valley we passed the night and the next day, during which it rained, rendering it quite uncomfortable, for the water soaked through my old poncho, which was not high enough from the ground for me to sit up straight in and not long enough to shelter over half of my body lying down. In this dilemma I was obliged to remain, crouching down in the daytime and cramped up at night. I knew it couldn't rain forever even in Virginia and I had faint hopes of being able to keep my head above water till it dried up. I succeeded in doing so and now have the satisfaction of seeing the sunshine again.

On Saturday the seventeenth we left the valley and moved a short distance in the direction of White House, a beautiful piece of property belonging to the wife of General Robert E. Lee, where we remained till Monday, establishing ourselves finally at Tunstall Station on the York and Richmond railroad.

CHAPTER 16.

Camping near Hanover.

Early on the twenty-first of May, 1862, the trumpet sounded the call to "strike tents" and fifteen minutes later everything was packed up and wagons loaded to start. An hour later the trumpet sounded again and off we started across a field of tall grass, over the railroad track to a hill just deserted by a regiment of Union cavalry. Here we halted for a while to allow the advance regiment to go ahead and then we passed over a hard, dry road, slowly and cautiously, making little progress, and halted in the afternoon about five or six miles from Cold Harbor.

It had been the intention of uniting the armies of McDowell and McClellan but the plans of the General and the War Department did not harmonize. McClellan said, "A telegram from the Secretary of War informed me that McDowell would advance from Fredericksburg and directed me to extend the right of the Army of the Potomac, to establish communications with him. I now proceeded to do all in my power to insure success on the new line of operation. On May twenty-four a telegram from the President informed me that McDowell would certainly march on the twenty-sixth and the very same day I was officially informed that the movement of McDowell was suspended."

About three o'clock in the afternoon of the twenty-fourth we received orders to move back over the road in the direction from whence we came. The rain poured in torrents and the beautiful road became a mudhole. We proceeded over the road for about two miles and turned to the left, passing a little village called Hanover, encamping a little way beyond. The next morning about ten o'clock we received a hasty order to "Fall in with muskets and canteens" which was afterward altered to include everything, but after pulling our ponchos down the order was countermanded. We are farthest in advance on this road and the enemy seems not far off. Last night they drove in our pickets for some distance and the preparation this morning may have been made on that account.

May twenty-sixth, 1862. Here I sit this morning in the entrance of my tent, still wet with the heavy dew of last night, which hangs in large beads upon the black cover, and rests like a fuzzy mist upon the leaves of clover. We are "living in clover" here for we occupy a large field of it, near a beautiful country residence, which is almost concealed from view by a magnificent grove of lofty trees, that rise majestically, spreading their wide branches over the garden around it. The house belongs to a stout old fellow named Johnson, who was last night visible for the first time, at the gate with his family, where they had been attracted by the music of our band. A young daughter who looks quite pretty from a distance is swinging on the gate like a child. The fence is covered with coats and blankets beginning to steam in the yet moderate heat of the rising sun. A little bird perched on top of one of these coats is carolling merrily. In a distant part of the field can be seen a number of cows quietly grazing in the tall, luxuriant grass. "Coffee is ready," so they say, so I'll close my book and hurry to the cook and get my coffee without delay.

CHAPTER 17.

Battle of Hanover Court House.

In the afternoon of May twenty-six, 1862, our company fell in for picket duty with knapsacks and haversacks and canteens. The sky, so clear and bright in the morning, became dark and threatening. Just as we were ready to start, the rain descended in torrents and we were soon wet through. Sergeant Fortesque and myself with nine others were sent to the extreme left of the line near an insignificant looking house and placed on duty there. As soon as I had posted my first relief of three men, I went in search of water and found a little spring behind the house. As soon as it became dark we extinguished our fires and lay quietly down on the wet grass to sleep. I was not sleepy, however, and lay for sometime in the pelting rain, watching the phosphorescent light of the little fireflies, shining here and there like little stars, emitting temporary flashes of light in the darkness like little diamonds in a cave. I had just dropped like a half-drowned rat into the arms of Morpheus when I was aroused by the sergeant and ordered to return to the camp.

The officer of the picket guard had been ordered to be ready to march with the regiment in the morning. We returned therefore about two miles in the direction of the camp and remained there in the mud growling and grumbling and laughing and joking at our own misery. In the morning as soon as objects around us began to be distinguishable, we marched back on the flooded road to the camp, which we reached tired, almost worn out with the leaden weight of our soaked knapsacks. The men were already falling in for the march, fortunately without knapsacks, and we were immediately hurried off again, without our coffee. The regiment of Lancers attached to Warren's brigade took the lead and we marched about eight miles under a supposition that we were simply going on a reconnaissance. We then, however, heard the dull booming of cannon ahead, which gradually grew louder and louder as we advanced, and bye and bye we could hear the rattling of small arms in the intervals as if there were a battle in progress somewhere in the distance. It had an invigorating effect on the men, who splashed through the mud and water with an elastic step as fresh as if they had just emerged from their tents after a good night's sleep. On we went over the muddy road, animated by the sound, and mile after mile was traversed without a murmur. It seemed, however, as if we would never reach the place of conflict. Leaving the road we turned to the left, crossed a field and mounted a hill where the roaring of artillery became more distinct at every discharge and every step brought us nearer to the sound.

We passed a house and marched through a beautiful garden, treading on the beauties of nature, so artistically arranged in beds, and I snatched some rosy-cheeked strawberries growing beside a fence. On we went over the field to a wood which was enveloped in the smoke of artillery which had just shaken the earth with its terrific noise. The sounds were no longer heard and the woods that a moment ago had echoed and re-echoed with the noise were now hushed and still; nothing heard but the heavy breathing of the heated men, and the rotten sticks cracking beneath their feet. This wood had been the scene of conflict for the trees were broken with shot and splintered with shell. The path was lined with cast-away knapsacks, haversacks and canteens whose marks identified them as belonging to the enemy. We emerged from the wood upon an open plain and we here saw our troops, regiment after regiment in hot pursuit of the flying enemy. Horsemen were galloping to and fro and we learned from them that they had a pretty brisk skirmish in which the enemy had been defeated and obliged to "skedaddle."

The head of the column had now overtaken a portion of the enemy's rear guard and the artillery was again at work shelling the woods on the right of a road running through the field. No sooner did we reach the wood in question than a heavy firing was heard in our rear and it was evident that the enemy had made a flank movement to the right and attacked our rear. It was a brilliant move and excellently well executed, but was made a little too quick and lost about half of its intended effect, for a courier on horseback rode hastily along the line and the regiments were turned quickly to the right about and marched back to the point of attack. The battle now began in earnest and the roaring of the artillery, the constant rattling of musketry and the loud yells and shouts of the combatants were terrific. We formed and advanced in line of battle through a field of tall, heavy-headed grain.

The Connecticut regiment was advancing to our left and to the left of them the artillery was posted, blazing rapidly away into the woods. A fine, noble-looking officer rode along the line in front of our regiment and asked us if we would not give the boys, who had been having some pretty hard work, "a good cheer." We acquiesced with a heartiness creditable to our lungs and it was taken up and repeated from battalion to battalion till it went the rounds of the whole army.

Our Colonel, Duryee, who was as cool and calm as if on evening parade, was ordered to proceed to the right. The battalion was quietly faced about and after proceeding a short distance entered the woods in line of battle, scrambling over fences and ditches, dodging between trees, pressing through brambles and briars and stumbling over fallen logs. The firing became more rapid and noisy. We made a detour to the left, passing several regiments, and were received by them with exclamations of delight mingled with words of encouragement. They had evidently withstood a terrific fire for the trees around were fairly riddled, the bark torn off in strips. Many prisoners were being brought in, some of them fine-looking fellows. We passed around to where the firing a few minutes ago was very fierce but now dying away and receding. Here in this path lay the Confederates that fell in the last fire, the most horrid images of blood and death.

One young fellow had fallen in the act of ramming his musket, for he held the ramrod, which was inserted half way into the barrel, with the bloodless fingers of his right hand, while his left hand grasped the barrel with the rigid grip of death. He lay upon his right side with his body bent slightly forward. His eyes were open and fixed with a glassy stare upon the barrel of his gun. Near by was a tall, stout, young man lying upon his back, his shoulders raised upon his knapsack and his head resting upon the roll, his eyes apparently looking at the sky to which his spirit had taken its flight. His hands were crossed upon his breast as if in sleep. He, and many others who had fallen, lay so close that it was difficult to step without treading upon them. In trying to avoid this, I trod upon the side of a little hillock, thick with glutinous blood, causing me to slip and almost tread upon one whose life had gushed out of an ugly wound behind his ear.

Here was one shot through the head, with his knees drawn up in the death agony, his light felt cap partly removed from his shattered skull and half filled with blood and brains. Another close by had his upper lip shivered with a musket ball, mouth and nostrils filled with coagulated blood. One poor fellow was still alive, but breathing with great difficulty; part of his head had been blown away and his quivering brain was exposed. Blood was trickling down his forehead into his eyes, which were rolling in agony, and his head was nodding at every pulsation of his laboring heart. It was a horrible sight and I longed to be able to alleviate his suffering. Death brought peace that night and he was buried in the morning.

The prisoners, guarded by Union soldiers, passed us, bearing in a blanket, with the tenderness of a brother, a wounded comrade who was moaning piteously with pain. A little farther on we emerged from the wood onto the road and here I caught a glimpse of the retreating enemy. Regiments of infantry were blazing away all around us as we advanced and a battery of artillery followed us, firing rapidly in the direction of our retreating foes. A staff officer rode by our side and a jolly, good-natured Brigadier called to him as he passed, "That's right, you take up the zoo-zoos in advance and I'll come along and we'll make a finish of this day's business to our entire satisfaction." On we went, crossing the railroad track and into a field in line of battle to meet the enemy. Our regiment was the farthest in advance on the field of battle at Hanover Court House, but the sun was rapidly descending the western sky and the enemy skedaddling too fast for us to catch them.

We remained about half an hour resting on the field and then after sending up cheer after cheer for our victory we returned and again passed the wood where the Confederate dead lay so close together.

It was dark when we halted for the night and I was too tired to get anything to lie down upon. The ground was wet and marshy and we were still damp from the drenching we received. I stretched myself upon the ground and was soon fast asleep. I awoke several times shivering and shaking but, exhausted as I was, soon fell asleep again. The next morning, May 28, Phoebus arose from his bed in the east and started on his journey drying up the dewdrops. Our damp clothes and the wet ground soon smoked beneath the rays of "Old Sol" and when he reached the zenith they were dry again.

The prisoners that were taken during the battle, about four hundred in number, were brought to our camp and placed under guard of our regiment and I had a chance to converse with many of them, finding nearly all anxious for the war to cease. They were North Carolinians, tired and sick of the fratricidal war. They belonged to the brigade of General Branch and spoke bitterly of their General.

The right wing of our regiment, accompanied by a squad of lancers, went out scouring the country during the morning, bringing in twenty-six additional prisoners. The number of dead and prisoners would probably be little less than seven hundred. Our loss in killed, wounded and missing was said to have been three hundred and ninety-seven.

Early in the morning a detail was sent out to bury the Confederate dead, who were placed in a pit and covered with dirt. They were North Carolinians pressed into the service of the Southern Confederacy fighting for the "old North State."

"They sleep 'neath the pines of a far-distant state,
They're buried by those who were foemen of late;
But the hearts of those foemen throb for the dead
And they whisper a prayer for the souls that have fled."

CHAPTER 18.

Losses from disease.

May twenty-nine, eighteen sixty-two. The Connecticut and our regiment and lancers with a battery of artillery started on a reconnaissance in the direction of Ashland. We were under the command of Colonel Warren, as brave a man as ever strode a steed. At this time he was acting Brigadier-General. We marched about six miles over a road covered with articles of clothing thrown away by the enemy, but we only succeeded in capturing eight of the enemy's cavalry in the expedition. Two of these were from North Carolina and the rest Virginians, the latter determined when released to fight again.

Our scouts in this expedition met the scouts of McDowell who was advancing to form a junction with McClellan. On our return, in passing the wood where the battle was fought, I noticed a hillock of new earth over which was an uneven piece of board nailed to a stake bearing the rough inscription "25 North Carolinians." On the other side of the road there were a number of little board headstones placed side by side bearing number and name of regiment of Federal dead. When we reached camp we found all the regiments had packed up and marched away. About four o'clock we started back to camp at Old Church near Johnson's house, which we reached about one o'clock next morning.

About two o'clock in the morning of the thirty-first we started forward again, reaching our old camp near Cold Harbor. There was a terrible battle in progress somewhere, which we could hear, and we were ordered to hold ourselves in readiness to march at a moment's notice. Our services were not required, however, in the battle of the Chickahominy. June first we rejoined our division under General Sykes which we found encamped on a hill.

June fifth, eighteen sixty-two. Here we are encamped in the woods among the wood ticks and black spiders with a canopy of green leaves over our heads, half concealing the blue sky, and a carpet of dry, rustling ones beneath our feet. I ramble around through the thick shrubbery and startle the little birds who flap their tiny wings and fly before me, quickly retreating as I advance, stopping long enough on every limb to whistle a defiant "Catch me if you can." How nimbly they flit from bough to bough and how saucily they bend their cunning little heads to wink with small, beadlike eyes. How beautiful they are, how graceful in every movement, how sweet in every song.

The other day, on evening parade, McClellan's short, concise proclamation was read to our brigade and at its conclusion General Sykes addressed us as follows: "Soldiers of New York and Connecticut: You have heard what our Commander-in-Chief McClellan says. I only add if there is any hard work to be done you have got to do it." This short Spartanlike speech was greeted with three rousing cheers and the men returned to their respective camps, expecting to be led against the enemy the next day. The next day came, however, without any orders to move.

A great many men are on the sick list and the regiment that left Baltimore with nine hundred men has been reduced to but little over half that number. The cause of this effect, or as Polonius says, "The cause of this defect," is the need of proper shelter and wholesome food. Our ponchos are worn out and our rations of musty crackers and canned beef weaken instead of nourish the men. We all feel the effect and are so weak we can hardly stand. One by one they are falling off. How many bereaved and broken-hearted mothers are mourning over the loss of dearly loved children who have fallen so early, like unripe fruit from the tree of life shaken by the simoons of the South? How many fond brothers and sisters will weep for those who have willingly offered themselves as a sacrifice on the altar of patriotism? Almost every day, when the roll is called in the different companies, some familiar name elicits no response and when repeated by the sergeant, someone in the ranks answers for his absent comrade "Sick in his tent." At each successive roll call the same answer is given; his familiar face is missed by his companions around the camp fire in the evenings.

The next we hear, "He is in the hospital." Later on we hear, "He is dead." Such thoughts were in my mind last night as I lay on my leafy bed with the silver light of the pale moon forcing its way through the tall treetops upon my uncovered head pillowed upon my hard haversack. I little thought a year ago that I would ever lay my wearied limbs upon the hard, cold ground. I do, however, and sleep as easy on the "flinty couch of war" as the rich merchant on his bed of down. I sleep in peace to be awakened by the stirring drum to attend the morning roll. But I am not happy and long for home. Will this war ever cease? I cannot find a satisfactory answer.

When McClellan took supreme command, they argued that he, energetic and enterprising, would end the war in ninety days, but the prophecy has been unfulfilled. It needed then but the fall of Manassas to end the war, the taking of eastern Tennessee and western Virginia to take away supplies, the fall of New Orleans, Nashville and Norfolk, the reduction of Yorktown and Corinth to give secession the "coup de grace," but the conflict still rages. "The fall of Richmond," according to these prophets, "will be the end," a "consummation devoutly to be wished." The question is, will they submit then or will they stubbornly fight it out beyond, turning the rich fields into fields of blood?

CHAPTER 19.

Review.

June seventh, eighteen sixty-two. The Tenth Regiment, McChesney's Zouaves, joined our brigade today and encamped in the woods near us. I heard one of them singing

> "Some love to roam o'er the dark sea foam
> Where the wild winds whistle free,
> But a chosen band in a mountain land
> And a life in the woods for me."

I couldn't help thinking as I listened how soon he'd change his tune. The fields are preferable to the woods for an encampment. Today while cool outside it is hot within and I believe Shadrach, Meshach and Abednego would acknowledge these woods to be like the "burning fiery furnace" of Nebuchadnezzar. Speaking of Neb., I have heard that this famous "King of the Jews" had "two pairs of stockings and two pairs of shoes." He was luckier than me, for my deeply furrowed shoes turn up at the toe, mutely appealing to be discharged from further service, while the stockings, the ragged-toed, odoriferous stockings, are in a rapid state of decomposition and decay. There is but a small remnant left for they have been pulled down and turned under so often that the leg of the sock no longer covers the ankle bone.

"The sweet South that breathes upon a bed of violets" according to the "Mobile Advertiser" wants a hero. This I, with Byron, consider "an uncommon want" when every month turns out a new one, who after filling the gazettes with cant, the age finds out is not the true one.

Beauregard, previous to the disastrous retreat from Corinth, was the hero of the South and they almost deified him into the demi-god of secession. He was considered the mighty man of the rebellion and was looked upon, I have no doubt, as equal to the ancient Hebrew warrors, three, who hearing David's wish, left the Cave of Adullam and broke through the army of the Philistines in the Valley of

Rephaim to bring water from the well of Bethlehem to quench David's thirst. This was their opinion of Beauregard before the battle of Corinth but opinions changed after the badly conducted affair. Who, now I wonder, will be the rising man?

June eight, eighteen sixty-two. This morning we were ordered to clean up for review. As no specified time was given, preparation was deferred by mutual consent until noon. I had stripped off my yellow-colored leggings, once a pure, milky white, to wash them for the occasion and was busily engaged dispatching my dinner when the unexpected order came to "Fall in." No time now to prepare, so we hurried off, presenting an exceedingly shabby appearance. The review took place in the open field and I believe it comprised the whole of General Porter's and General Sykes' divisions. One regiment in General Martindale's brigade, the First Michigan, presented quite a soldierly appearance. The Berdan Sharpshooters in uniforms of every conceivable color looked quite saucy, all having an easy, rollicking manner.

We were drawn up in one long line division front and awaited the appearance of the reviewing officer. Bye and bye a number of horsemen rode along the lines and two of them attracted particular attention, the first being a dark-complexioned man in a tight-fitting uniform extensively ornamented with gold trimming, wearing a cap of silver cloth with gold bands. On his breast he wore a cross and two or three gold stars. He proved to be the Spanish General Prim, ci-devant commander of the allied forces in Mexico, but now diplomatic plenipotentiary of Spain to that country. His campanion was dressed in a similar manner but his ornaments were silver instead of gold. They were introduced to Colonel Warren by General Sykes and made some remarks, the only word which we could understand being the well-known word Zouaves. After cordially shaking hands with our Colonel he passed on to view the other regiments, stopping to compliment the colonel of each. On his return he requested us to remain and execute the bayonet exercise, which we did apparently to his satisfaction.

CHAPTER 20.

A visit to the picket guard.

Soon after we returned from the review, Healy, better known on account of his light hair as "Whitey Bob," entered the camp with a haversack full of cakes, exposed temptingly to view, as if purposely to make our mouths water. He had come across in his travels, a sutler, who in consideration of a quid pro quo had parted with part of his large supply of cakes. I resolved to go for some, with Brazzoni. We went through the camp of the Connecticut First and crossed on some rails over the little brook beyond, passing afterward in succession the different camps of Regulars till we reached the headquarters of General Sykes. In the distance we could see two large tents which Brazzoni proclaimed to be sutlers. We crossed the field, accelerating our pace at the pleasing sight, and were soon mingling with the eager crowd of hungry soldiers around the door. Unfortunately, he had no more cakes but did have almond and hazel nuts and as I had come to purchase something I resolved to buy some. I invested a dollar, for it was a pleasure to spend money where money is hard to spend. After walking about a mile we passed through a fine peach orchard, the property of Dr. Gaines, whose palatial residence on the top of the hill beyond was one of the most magnificent and beautifully situated places in the country. It reminded me of the beautiful structures along the banks of the Hudson and at Ravenwood where the merchant princes of New York pass the summer. Dr. Gaines had his horse harnessed, when the Federal troops arrived, ready to start and expressed the hope that the Federal army would be sunk in the water of the Chickahominy that runs swiftly along on the edge of his vast domain. On the opposite side of the road the red hospital flag of the Union army now waves over one or two of his outhouses; the doors being open, the groans and agonizing cries of the wounded can be heard. The poor fellows lie upon the hard floor beneath their blankets and the wind outside sighs in sympathy. About half a mile from Gaines' house the shallow waters of the dark river rush through the trees and bushes and tangled briars and go meandering through the bed of the valley. Over this stream our army has built three pontoon bridges within sight of each other and our men are now busily engaged constructing corduroy roads over the swamps beyond. We found our men stationed on the central bridge with a line of pickets extending a short distance in the swamp beyond, some of them obliged to stand in water up to their waists. The enemy pickets were posted in the woods close by. General Porter rode down to the bridge with the Spanish general and ordered our men to begin firing. The enemy pickets fell back at the first firing; they had the advantage, sheltered by the tall trees, while our men were obliged to run the risk of being shot or crouch down in the swamp grass and run the risk of drowning. General Sykes had a narrow escape, for while he was reconnoitering the woods with an opera glass on the opposite side of the bridge, a ball whistled over his shoulders close to his head. He is a brave man, for he never flinched but continued his observation as if nothing had happened.

When I reached the bridge one of our men on picket in the water fired his piece at a bold soldier in the woods, who returned the compliment, the ball striking the water a little short of our man's head, who dodged like a duck. A little while after four men from the Connecticut First, while endeavoring to extend the line of pickets, were fired upon from the woods, but passed on unheeding the first shot, but several more caused them to drop out of sight in the tall sedge. The next morning as if by mutual consent the pickets of both sides appeared on the edge of the wood to exchange words instead of bullets.

CHAPTER 21

Battle of Gaines' Mill.

On the afternoon of Friday, the thirteenth of June, 1862, I was aroused from my siesta and ordered to get ready to march in light marching order as soon as possible. The whole regiment was notified and fifteen minutes later we were marching up the road. About a quarter of a mile from camp we were conducted across a field and drawn up in line of battle on the edge of a wood. We were next ordered to lie down and await further orders. The bright, golden sun was gradually descending in the silver-colored, cloudless sky and the air was hot and close. There was a gentle zephyr breeze, but too feeble to move the stately pines and barely stirred the topmost branches. The calm, still air was vocal with the noise of little chirping insects and a solitary bird could be heard above the insect's hum. The sun shone on the greasy faces of the bronzed soldiers, streaming with sweat.

Our Colonel, Duryee rode along the line of his crouching Zouaves to keep them down in their places, and the men began to speculate in whispers on the enemy making an attempt to turn our right. Bye and bye a messenger galloped across the field to our Colonel and we were soon once more on the road, coming to a halt in front of the lancer's encampment. The Confederates had appeared in force at Old Church, where they had attacked the Fifth Regular Cavalry, cutting to pieces four companies of that regiment, and we were sent in a round-about way to cut off their retreat. We halted at Old Church for the night and started forward again before daylight, the enemy having boldly taken the road toward White House. We followed in pursuit back to Tunstall Station where we discovered traces of their march. They had escaped us, having made the circuit of the whole army, from the right wing, around the left, burning and destroying everything they came across in their progress. This was the boldest exploit that has been made during the war. The next day we marched back to camp, having been completely outwitted by the daring enemy.

June twenty, eighteen sixty-two. About twelve o'clock today while we were quietly sipping our soup and champing our biscuit the Confederates opened on our camp and a ball went whizzing over our heads, quickly followed by another, and a third fell into camp, passing through a tent, shattering the thigh and hip bone of a young man named Matthews. The poor fellow, mangled and bleeding, lay upon the ground, unconscious for a few moments, then opened his eyes and inquired in a feeble, plaintiff manner "Where am I?" There was something so very touching in that little question, so calm, so low and yet so distinct that it stirred the fountains of pity in my heart and it was with difficuly I kept the tears from gushing from my eyes, and I could read in the countenances of my comrades how quickly the rugged heart of the soldier can be moved and softened by the sight of the pale face, the bloodless lip and the pitiful voice of a dying comrade. How true is the expression "One touch of pity makes the whole world kin." The hard heart melts in pity at the sight of suffering humanity although a struggle is made to repress any outward manifestation of all that is Godlike for fear of being considered weak.

When the dying man was informed that he was in the camp, an expression of wonder crossed his face and he asked if a Confederate had hit him. It seemed as if he could scarcely realize that he was struck in his own camp, three miles away from the enemy. "I feel better now but my lips burn so," he said. "I wish you would wet them with water." These were his last words.

June twenty-six, eighteen sixty-two. Heavy firing was heard on the right during the afternoon and about six o'clock we received orders to advance in that direction. Coming to a halt we were drawn up in line of battle behind long lines of troops drawn up in the same way, reaching straight ahead as far as the eye could reach. Firing continued almost incessantly until dark and we lay down in our places expecting to advance in the morning, but instead at first break of dawn June twenty-seven, we marched back to camp and after slinging our knapsacks started back toward Cold Harbor. Halting on a hill, we could distinctly hear the sounds of cannon already at work and apparently approaching. The Tenth was drawn up on our left and we lay down and quietly awaited the enemy advance. The sun was boiling hot and the atmosphere close and sultry. Army wagons, artillery and ambulances were confusedly jumbled up in our rear, possibly to cover up the retreat of the right wing under Porter. An officer informed Warren that the enemy already had possession of our deserted camp, also the tents and knapsacks of Company B who were out on picket duty.

We had been upon the top of the hill about fifteen or twenty minutes when the firing began again and gradually approached. I kept my eyes fixed upon the open space in the direction of Cold Harbor and soon saw the pickets slowly falling back and firing in retreat; sometimes they halted to fire and finally fell back to a little rivulet where we were stationed. The artillery firing that we heard advancing now turned off and rattled furiously down through the woods and soon volleys of musketry mingled with the sound. Bye and bye I saw a single horseman appear, and another, and another, and soon several wheeled around in the open space and the sunlight flashed on the polished surface of a brass fieldpiece. It was the enemy planting his cannon and he had selected a splendid position for his battery. "See, see," I said, "they are planting their cannon." "Those are our cannon," said Sergeant Fortesque. "You don't suppose they would allow the enemy to place their piece there, do you?" "Bang!" went the loud report, down went the battalion and directly over our heads whistled the terrible engine of death. Fortesque arose out of the dust, his face pale and fixed with an anxious look. We had a battery on the right, one on the left and one on the hill in the rear and all three opened on the bold and daring enemy, who returned the first with great spirit and skill. Every gun was exceedingly well managed and every shot and shell fell with great accuracy almost in the midst of our crouching battalion. One made a peculiar kind of noise like a humming top whenever it burst. Solid shot struck the bank on which we lay and flopped spitefully around, turning end over end through the air, which was musical with the whistling shot and bursting shell. Some of the men buried their heads, others made barricades of the knapsacks, some laughed and joked, others looked serious and said nothing.

Lieutenant-Colonel Duryee, mounted on his handsome black charger, disdained to dodge the shot which fell around him like hail, some of them falling in the mud, splashing it thirty or forty feet in the air. The enemy seemed determined to make a target of him, for almost every shot went whistling close to his head, making his escape seem miraculous. After the artillery fire had continued nearly an hour the Confederate guns suddenly ceased to roar. An awful silence now ensued only broken by the rattling of the artillery leaving its position and a thrilling whisper went through the battalion that the enemy was about to charge. I raised my head and sure enough there came the rebel infantry, their bayonets glistening in the sun over the tops of the bushes on the opposite side of the ravine.

The clear, distinct voice of our Colonel could be heard from one end of the line to the other, encouraging his men and keeping them informed of the enemy's movements. "They are as yet on the opposite side of the ravine; fire low and take deliberate aim; don't get excited, and when you charge be careful to keep the ranks closed. The fire will be by company, and be careful to reserve your fire till you get the command. They are now crossing the ravine." "Shall I order the battalion to close after they fire, sir?" These words were addressed to Colonel Warren, who answered in the negative, giving as a reason that the enemy was advancing in double column. "They are now deploying on this side of the ravine," continued the colonel, again addressing the men. "Fire low and don't waste a cartridge. Here they come! Attention! Forward, march!" At the command the men started to their feet, kicking the knapsack barricades out of the way, and when the second was given, the battalion moved forward in line of battle to the top of the hill, receiving as it advanced a perfect shower of bullets. Reaching the top we were ordered to halt and fire by company—"Battalion ready, commence firing." Discharge after discharge belched out in quick succession and the enemy fell back discomfited into the bushes. The enemy artillery, witnessing their infantry repulse, opened on us with grapeshot, which caused us to flop down on our faces again in the dust. Here we lay panting in the sun, partly from heat and partly from excitement, and the swinging noise of grape, more musical than agreeable, was followed by rifle shot and shell.

Our batteries, having taken up a new position in the rear opened fire again over our heads and it was difficult to distinguish the fire of our friends from that of our enemy. Never before did I hear such an infernal roar of artillery. Fancy five or six cannon belching away at the same time and five or six shells bursting simultaneously in the air. The noise was terrific and the ground fairly trembled.

Sergeant Marsh of our company approached the colonel with an anxious look. He wished to procure a stretcher for Sergeant Phillips, who was badly wounded in the neck. "Is anyone else hurt?" I asked. He replied, "Deely is dead." I involuntarily cast my eyes toward the right, and sure enough Deely was lying on his back, his pale face still retaining in death his habitually good-natured smile. Little "Body" was struck by a buckshot and a ball struck the ground between the two men on my left, scattering the dirt and almost blinding us with dust.

Company I was ordered to crawl up in advance on the top of the hill. Again the enemy emerged from the bushes and attempted to advance and again we met them with a hot fire, forcing them to retire. Again the enemy opened with grapeshot and again we buried our noses in the dirt. Each shot fell closer, many of them dropping in our midst, and the place becoming too hot, we were ordered after retaining the position for two whole hours to move to the left, where we were again drawn up in line of battle to await the enemy's approach.

The road was cut quite deep into the embankment and we were obliged to clamber up the sides to watch the enemy approach. While we were thus occupied, someone informed Major Hull, who was much interested in the welfare of the wounded, that Phillips had been abandoned on the field.

"That must not be," said he. "He must be brought off."
A call was made for volunteers and a dozen men answered
to the call. Paul Glyman Tibout and a companion went for
the wounded man.

Our batteries which had retired still further back and
taken up a new position opened a deadly fire upon the enemy who was again advancing over the field we had just
left. Some of the shells exploded over our heads, killing
three of our men and wounding Lieutenant Cartwright.
Colonel Duryee spoke to Colonel Warren about it and he
was told that "such things could not be helped where the
opposing parties were so close together" and he was advised "not to mind it as it was a good American battery
of Napoleon guns," as if it were an honor to be killed by
such a battery and such guns, even if they were our own.
Colonel Duryee couldn't see it, and moved his battalion a
little to the left on the road in a hollow where the men were
obliged to stand in the water of a pond up to their knees.
The enemy was advancing in line of battle across the field
and we were ordered to advance and meet them. Over we
went through the swamp, which was very deep in some
places, causing considerable confusion. Men were sepa-
rated from their respective companies but fell in wherever
they happened to be and we advanced in line of battle across
the field. Ascending a little hillock with our colors raised
high in the air we caught sight of the enemy and the firing
commenced. Whiz, whiz, went the balls, and the men
began to fall quite rapidly around me. The line faltered
for a moment and then was closed up and with terrific
yells we advanced upon the foe. Corporal Olivia, one of
the color corporals, leaped high in the air and fell dead
in front of the colors, and another Corporal whirled around
and fell dead behind him. In the hasty glance I cast around
I saw among many other familiar faces the pale face of
Corporal Ryer of our company lying with face upturned,
dead. Mandeville and O'Neil, too, had fallen. Many of
our little company lay scattered around upon the ground
moaning in agony with ghastly wounds. On we had to go
over their prostrate bodies, firing as we went and receiving
fire in return. Lieutenant Agness fell, wounded in the
breast, and I nearly stumbled over him in his fall. Soon

we had the satisfaction of seeing the enemy give way, we following after them yelling like hounds. In the place where we first saw the enemy the field was marked by a long line of Confederate dead and wounded, in proof of our good marksmanship, many poor fellows groaning with agony. I stooped down while we were advancing and sprinkled a few drops of water from my canteen on the tongue of a wounded Confederate and I never shall forget the look of gratitude he gave me. He tried to speak but his tongue refused its office. I interpreted the few inarticulate sounds for "I thank you, sir." His eyes said these words more plainly than his tongue could have spoken and I felt pleased that I had been able to perform an act of kindness on the battlefield.

We followed the retreating enemy across the field to a clump of pines and then the reason was apparent for their falling back, for out of the woods a galling fire of musketry was opened on us and the woods seemed to be fairly alive with Confederate soldiery. A bullet whistled unpleasantly close to my nose and another passed my leg, and I perceived we were in a very unenviable situation. A battery opened on us at the same time and the firing became more rapid and furious than I had ever heard it before at any time during the war. We maintained our ground, however, until we were relieved and we then fell back to reform the remnant of the regiment. While resting, about a quarter of a mile from where we made the charge, Colonel Warren came down and ordered us forward again to protect his battery, which was threatened, being in position and pegging away from the top of a hill directly in the rear of the place where we made the charge. We were ordered to sit down in our places to await further orders. We had hardly seated ourselves, before the enemy who had been firing shot and shell at the battery opened on us with grape which whistled around through the air like hail. First one, then two, three, and soon a whole battalion of our soldiers came flying over the top of a hill, some without hats, some without muskets, and all without courage; mouths and eyes wide open, panting for breath. "What's the matter," said some of our men, "are we getting the worst of it?" But no answer was given. The grapeshot was for them, although we were obliged to share it and more of our boys fell under the murderous fire than the cowards who were running away from it.

In the midst of the storm of lead and hail the clear, calm voice of Colonel Duryee was heard calling "Attention!" then the order "Forward, march!" and away we went to the top of the hill to meet the exultant enemy and check its victorious advance. The order seemed cruel, but the move was necessary to counteract the panic which seemed to be taking possession of our troops. The valley was filled with an impenetrable smoke like a dense fog and nothing for a little while could be seen but fire belching from the guns in various parts of the field. The noise was terrific, shaking the hills and reverberating through the valley, but loud above all was the exultant, fiendlike yell of the Confederate soldiers. Nearer and nearer the sounds approach and now the smoke in front of us partly clears away, revealing a Confederate regiment not a stone's throw from our battalion, steadily advancing on our battery. The white battle flag with blood-red cross, waves defiantly under our very noses and yet some our men cry out that we are firing upon our own friends and nearly the whole battalion ceases firing, while the advancing friends, as proof of their friendship, pour volley after volley into our thin ranks. Tim Russell falls badly wounded at my side and Jimmie Mahoney tumbles headlong to the ground in front and Farrell Levitt and myself are struck almost simultaneously but neither of us badly wounded. Mine is nothing at all, a lump on the wrist from a spent ball, and I returned to the fight just in time to hear Colonel Warren say in an excited and emphatic tone of voice, "They are not our men, blaze away into them, boys." We did blaze away and they into us and through the smoke I could see that they had come to a halt. It was a brave regiment, for although they did not advance, they held their ground under our murderous fire, when to all appearance they did not have a hundred men left to fight.

I heard the battery on the left leaving the field and looking in that direction I saw regiment after regiment of Confederate infantry advancing on us from that flank. Our artillery, that we were supporting, then fell back and I must confess I felt relieved when I heard the Colonel command "About face." We retreated slowly in line of battle, halting and turning on the top of every hillock long enough to pour another volley on our advancing foes. On one of these occasions I stood between two little bushes and fired, when I heard Sweeny behind me saying "That's right," and stepping aside at his request to let him take a shot, he was instantly shot down as if by lightning and rolled to the bottom of the hill. A second before I had occupied that spot, and had I remained there a second longer I would not have lived to write this record.

It was now rapidly getting dark and we were glad at the approaching close of the contest. We fell back so slowly and deliberately that the enemy in the dusk, succeeded in getting his cannon on our right flank and while we were behind a hill, watching for him in front he sent an enfilading shot down the gully along the whole line, fortunately, a little too high for mischief. Had it been leveled a few inches lower it would probably have killed over half of what remained of the regiment. Colonel Duryee was concerned for the safety of his men and told Warren that if his regiment remained where they were much longer he would not have men enough left to go on guard. "How many are left?" asked Warren, seeming to manifest a stoical indifference for his own or his soldiers' lives, having a total disregard for death himself. "About a hundred and fifty," said Duryee, "and half of them are out of cartridges, and the others too exhausted to fire." "Well," said Warren, "I'll go and see Sykes." He soon returned and ordered us once more to fall back. On the road a little way from our last halting place stood a large house into which the enemy sent a rifle cannon ball as we were passing, knocking boards and splinters all over us. This was the last shot fired in the battle of Gaines' Mill for it was now too dark to continue operation. We held the valley and the enemy the battle field. Had we been driven half a mile further, the long bridge over the Chickahominy would have been in the possession of the enemy and the whole of Porter's corps would have been killed or captured. Porter lost in this fight seven thousand men, our regiment alone, losing in killed and wounded two hundred and seventeen.

Just beyond the mutilated house we halted and sank down on the ground so tired and exhausted that many fell asleep. We could see the enemy moving around on the field searching with lanterns for their wounded friends. We expected to remain and receive a new attack next morning, but thank heaven, we were mistaken, for about an hour later we were removed about half a mile further back and allowed to sleep in the marsh near the Chickahominy.

Colonel Gouverneur Kemble Warren (left). Through his efforts the 5th New York became one of the best-drilled units in the Federal service. [Brian C. Pohanka Collection] Lieutenant Colonel Hiram Duryea (right), who commanded the Zouaves at the battle of Gaines's Mill, was a strict disciplinarian. One soldier called him "as brave a man as ever stood in shoe-leather." [New York Division of Military and Naval Affairs]

CHAPTER 22.

Battle of Malvern Hill.

About one o'clock in the morning, June 28, 1862, we were aroused, and we quietly crossed a long bridge of sand through the swamp, then over a wooden bridge over the river to the other side, where we halted again and slept until morning. Our troops burned the wooden bridge to prevent pursuit by the enemy. Early in the morning several shots were fired and the regiment was drawn up for action. Captain Lewis of Company D said, "We must hold this position if it costs the life of every man in this reserve." Believing a big fight imminent, I threw away my heavy knapsack and prepared for action. We were conducted to the top of a hill overlooking the valley and our cannon was placed in position on the heights and we remained there till nightfall.

Crackers, coffee, bacon and vegetables were distributed and every one seemed to enjoy himself more than I had seen them do for some time. It seemed suspicious, this generosity with these articles, and more suspicious to leave so much behind when we left the spot. We marched forward quite a distance and then halted in a vast plain to receive the knapsacks which had been carried in the wagons. We were told not to try to pick out our own, but to take the first that came. Great fires were kindled and knapsacks without number were piled upon these fires and burnt to ashes. The men began to whisper, "It's a regular skedaddle."

The captain advised us previous to starting forward again "to be quiet if we got into another action and pay particular attention to orders." We noticed on every side deserted encampments and huge fires blazing; not a soldier to be seen; not a sound heard in the stillness of the night, except our own whispering and the tramping of our feet. Bye and bye we approached a large encampment and we could see the inmates quietly sleeping inside the tents, which reassured us and we felt that everything was all right after all. We changed our minds, however, at learning that this was Savage Station, the general hospital, filled with sick and wounded. We recrossed the Chickahominy at this place over a high bridge which was partially destroyed. We were ordered to have everything in readiness in case of an attack but we were not molested.

A little way beyond we came upon another vast plain, fairly covered with army wagons which appeared to be lightening their loads by casting away everything that they could not conveniently carry. Our duty was to protect these wagons for we were obliged to halt until they all passed forward on the road, the men in the meantime falling down in their places fast asleep at every stop.

It began to rain and the men began to grumble, worrying whether they were going to be obliged to march all night. They were obliged to march all night, and just at daylight were passing through White Oak Swamp. We marched with considerable caution and halted about eight o'clock on Charles City road. We were drawn up in line of battle and remained under arms all day, not daring to leave the spot.

No fires were allowed to be kindled to boil our coffee and it was exceedingly difficult to obtain even a drink of water. In the evening I was on picket guard and consequently got no more sleep than I did the night before. In the middle of the night when I was stumbling around in the woods to post my pickets, we were startled by the report of a rifle, then another and another and soon the whole regiment on our left seemed to be engaged with the enemy. In the confusion I heard the voice of the officer of the guard, calling in an excited voice for me to draw in my pickets, which I did at his command. The firing ceased, leaving everything still as death and I went back and posted my pickets again, but nearer to the guard reserve. Everything went on quietly till morning when the guard was drawn in and the regiment started forward again on its travels.

We reached, about noon, June 30, eighteen sixty-two, the succession of little hills known as Malvern Hill and took up a position in the woods. Pickets were thrown out and we remained under arms during the entire day, hearing the roaring of the cannon in the battle of White Oak Swamp which was then taking place. For four or five hours the sound seemed neither to advance or to recede but afterward every report came nearer and nearer and it was evident the foe was again driving our troops before them. Soon the battalion we had planted on the hill began to blaze away and then the gunboats on the James River opened fire, sending their huge shells screaming and shrieking through the air over our heads, tearing down the forest trees in the distance with a sound like rumbling thunder.

The firing was all on our side for a long time, for we had possession of every available place and the enemy was unable to use his guns. Several times it became evident that the enemy was trying to flank us in the woods for our guns blazed away among the trees, unpleasantly close, tearing limbs and rattling through the forest, and never before did I hear such a rapid fire and furious discharge of artillery. The gunboats continued to fire without intermission, then night set in and the cheers of our troops reverberated from hill to hill and from the boats and the report was circulated that we had cut "secesh" all to pieces. We were jubilant at this news and were permitted to light fires to boil our coffee. One half of the regiment went on picket duty and the other half lay down quietly to sleep. Next morning the whole regiment went on picket duty. About three o'clock in the afternoon the music of the artillery commenced again and soon after was mingled with the rattling of small arms which continued till dark.

Warren brought a section of his battery to work in the cornfield and the huge shells from the gunboats, in connection with his battery, two or three times drove back the enemy when they were endeavoring to turn this flank. Had they succeeded in doing so, the whole Army of the Potomac would have been lost. The gunboats saved the flank and thus saved the army. *Fiat justitia ruat caelum* and this acknowledgment is but doing simple justice to those gallant vessels, for we on this flank were in a position to know and appreciate the precariousness of our situation. "We have whipped them at all points," was whispered around as a result of the afternoon's work and the assertion was received with great satisfaction, but in the middle of the night we were aroused from sleep to sneak away from a badly whipped enemy in the dark. It was strange, wondrous strange, this movement, but I wisely kept my mouth shut. It was daylight before the whole army got away. The rain began to descend in torrents and we were soon drenched to the skin, weary, sleepy, dejected and almost despairing. The mud was deep and sticky and the marching exceedingly hard. Every where we halted the men fell down exhausted in their places and slept half buried in the mud and water.

Never did I see an army so dirty, so tired and so depressed in spirit before. In the evening we reached Harrison's Landing and there halted. Harrison's Landing could be defended on three sides by gunboats and our fears began to subside and we boasted that secesh would not dare to attack us there. I wrapped myself in my wet blanket and lay down in the mud and rain and slept as soundly as if I had been reposing on a feather bed.

CHAPTER 23.

The Rebecca of Pottstown.

August eleven, eighteen sixty-two. Forty-five days after the Battle of Gaines' Mill we struck our tents and prepared to march, no one knew where. All that we knew was that our knapsacks were to be carried in transports and from this we anticipated a long and wearisome march. While the men were busy filling canteens and the note of preparation was going on, the sergeant detailed me for duty at the adjutant's office and that I was to remain on the vessel with the regimental baggage to its destination. This information dispelled the dissatisfaction I at first felt, as the prospect of a sail instead of a long hard march was a relief. The sun was exceedingly hot and, dripping with perspiration, we followed the wagons to the landing. There were wagons innumerable and heaps upon heaps of knapsacks waiting for transportation. It took till after midnight to get everything on board. All the men marched back to the camp except two of us.

The boat was a barge or rather a canal boat, very long and narrow, very gloomy and deserted. The representative from the Tenth and I held a consultation as to sleeping quarters, and finally decided to seek a little of "tired nature's sweet restorer" in the hold. He laid his poncho, a new one, on a couple of rifle cases and we both lay down on it to sleep. My companion was bigger than I and the cases were narrow so I didn't get over a quarter of a ration of bed. I was sleepy enough, but could not sleep, for I was tormented by myriads of blood thirsty mosquitoes, singing their battle songs, butting each other's brains out in the dark. My companion, too, was troubled for he tossed and tumbled around on the rifle cases, flinging his arms around his head and bringing the palms of his hands in contact with his face with a ringing sound like the snap of a mule driver's whip. His uneasiness kept me in a constant state of suspense, for at every roll he nearly wedged me off the case. I drew my legs up, and thrust them down again, folded my arms and unfolded them, all to no purpose so gave up the idea of sleep in despair. I lay and listened to the squeaking of the mice and rats playing hide and seek around the boat, sometimes passing, in their innocent amusement, over my pedal extremities, causing me to give some vigorous kicks in the dark. In the morning I had the good fortune to fall into a little nap and when I awoke I had both cases at my disposal. Because of the narrowness and crowded condition of the boat it was somewhat difficult to navigate without tumbling into the water or into the hold. The man from the Tenth had already had his breakfast and directed me where I could prepare mine. The stove was rusty and the single link of pipe leaned over and smoked furiously.

The Rebecca of Pottstown, Pa., had a generally mutilated appearance and had evidently been constructed after the models I used to whittle out of chips, in my childhood, to navigate the mud puddles in the neighborhood of my father's house in New York City. Her splendid young captain was John Latham Comet Deitzwaller whose reserve melted away before the heat of our sociability. We lay at Jamestown about twenty hours, a place full of historical interest but rather insignificant in appearance. We were surprised when we reached the mouth of the James River to see its extraordinary width. At Newport News we saw the masts of a sunken vessel, and a big ocean steamer. In the evening the lights on the vessels was a magnificent sight. Then we sailed to Yorktown where Baker and I took a stroll through the town.

We soon reached the mouth of the Potomac, the clear blue river of such remarkable width and beautiful scenery on both sides. At Aquia Creek I went ashore and was left behind. A lieutenant on another boat gave me a pass to Washington. After arriving I walked up Pennsylvania Avenue, a fine street, found fine people. I went to Grover's theatre and saw John E. Owens in The Yankee Teamster, after which I sought shelter in an unfenced lot. In the morning, I performed my toilet at a pump, went in search of something to eat, then visited public buildings. While in Washington, I attended Ford's Theatre where I saw Maggie Mitchell. After some days I became impatient to return to the regiment and when the opportunity presented itself I did so.

CHAPTER 24.

The Second Battle of Bull Run.

Our regiment and the Tenth, known as the National Zouaves, fought close together at Groveton under Colonel Warren on August twenty-nine, eighteen sixty-two. The enemy, with a much greater army was in the woods and we tried to drive them out, but they forced our depleted ranks to retreat. Our officers and men resisted gallantly, many being killed and others made prisoners. The battle at its height was terrible as shells were hurled from every direction. The ground was gay with the uniforms of the fallen of our company.

A little Frenchman, a brave fellow, recently made a corporal and placed among the color guard, was killed while bravely endeavoring to bring off the colors of the regiment. Every one of the corporals and color sergeants was killed or wounded, and the flag, for the second time went down upon the bloody field, when the Frenchman wrenched it from the hands of the dead hero and proudly raised it aloft, just as a bullet pierced his own forehead and with a yell he leaped into the air and fell dead across the prostrate body of the other guardsman, half buried beneath the folds of the starry banner they both died to save, but the flag was not lost, for a stout heart and a strong arm raised the proud emblem from the dead body of the faithful Gaul and bore it in triumph from the field.

Sergeant Sovereign was a tall fine looking young man about twenty-three years of age, eager, ambitious, fond of distinction and brave to a fault. He was the son of well-to-do parents. After the battle of Gaines' Mill which cost us a number of valuable officers he was promoted to a lieutenancy and allowed thirty days' leave of absence. He procured a handsome uniform in New York and was certainly a splendid looking officer, returning to the regiment just in time to be killed in this second battle of Bull Run.

A few days after the battle we received permission from the enemy under a flag of truce, to revisit the field and remove the wounded which they were unable to care for. An old gentleman with gray hair, accompanied the party, and begged us piteously to assist him in searching through the heaps of slain for his son, his darling boy, but the boys were piling into the wagons, the moaning, groaning, wounded and could not stop to help search for the dead. The old gentleman wandered around in search of his bright boy, but could see nothing like a bright new uniform and was turning away when his eyes fell upon a naked body and at once he recognized the features of his son. His bright uniform was stripped off and carried away with his sword and ornamental belt. When he had returned from New York his father had accompanied him to the camp but no one knew where he was during the battle. Almost prostrated with grief, he tenderly buried his son on the field, with the help of some of his comrades.

Major Carlile Boyd, who as Captain and second in command of the Zouaves was severely wounded at Second Bull Run. Southwick tells how the men used to imitate Boyd's habit of tugging his moustache. [Brian C. Pohanka Collection]

On the field of the Second Battle of Bull Run, three monuments have been erected by the State of New York for the First, Fifth and Fourteenth Regiments. That for the Fifth is surmounted by the corps badge of the company, a large marble Maltese Cross. A large flagpole stands in front of the monument from which a flag is unfurled every day.

The monument bears the following inscription:

Erected by the State of New York, September 29, 1906, to commemorate the heroic service of the Fifth Regiment, New York Volunteer Infantry (Duryee Zouaves.) Here, about four p. m., August 30, 1862, the regiment, 462 strong, supported Hazlette's Battery D, Fifth U. S. Artillery, when attacked by a division of the victorious Confederates. The regiment stubbornly withstood this force, and checked its advance, until the battery had withdrawn. In holding this position the regiment suffered the greatest loss of life sustained by any infantry regiment, in any battle, during the entire Civil War.

The casualties were: Killed or mortally wounded, 124; wounded, 223. Both color-bearers and seven out of eight of the color-guards were killed, but the colors were brought with honor off the field.

CHAPTER 25.

Changes in Company F.

October twenty-three, eighteen sixty-two. Swartwout is yet I believe in the regular army. Absalom Wetmore, his successor, is at home sick, and Hagan is dead. We have no captain now to fill their places and Ensign Winslow, a brother of the Major, is now the only officer in command of the company.

October twenty-four, eighteen sixty-two. Brigadier-General Warren, ci-devant Colonel of the gallant Fifth, arrived in camp at dusk this evening; Lieutenants Formsbury and Parker also arrived during the day. Parker is First Lieutenant.

October thirty. We broke camp today and started off on the longest road to Harpers Ferry. We are now halting and will probably bivouac for the night in Pleasant Valley.

November first we crossed the waters of the rocky Potomac and the still more rocky Shenandoah at Harpers Ferry into Dixie. We are marching down one of the valleys of Virginia to meet Johnny Secesh who is rolling up his sleeves to receive us. We can hear at intervals the sullen boom of cannon on the distant hills. It is the premonitory muttering of the coming storm when the earth will shake beneath the shock of battle, the red lightning will flash from the mouths of thousands of brazen instruments of death, the besom of destruction sweep once more over the contending hosts and the bibulous earth suck up, once more, noble blood.

November two. We reached Snickersville tonight and were drawn up in line of battle near the village awaiting the enemy. The cannonading which we had heard all day seemed to be approaching nearer and nearer at every discharge and there seemed to be fair prospect of fight. We were very tired and consequently very unwilling to engage. After nightfall we were conducted to the top of the mountain where the fight had been, but it was too late to continue the skirmish. We slept on top of the cold, bleak hill on the road called Snickersgap to prevent the advance of the enemy.

November three. The enemy is reported in considerable force on the opposite side of the Shenandoah, daring us to advance. About three o'clock Carothers, who was then on guard, informed us that the enemy could be seen through a glass, coming through the valley below. We laughed at him and in vain he pointed to a great cloud of dust that, foglike, almost concealed the beautiful valley and winding river, as a proof of his assertion. In the midst of our raillery, however, two or three loud reports reached us from the valley and our Colonel as a precaution shifted our position a little further back.

On these "Grampian Hills" somebody's "father has recently fed his flocks," for the hills abound in sheep. Some are killed and dragged to the fire for roasting. There are plenty of rabbits too, giving great sport to our boys. Some of us went out foraging and secured a large supply of walnuts.

November fifth. A party of Confederates appeared again today in the valley but made no demonstration and soon disappeared. I had an unpleasant duty to perform, for I was acting sergeant of the guard and was obliged to arrest and detain stragglers from the other regiments left behind.

November six. We deserted the gap this morning and started off down the Loudon Valley, without disturbing our Southern friends in the Shenandoah Valley. We passed through the village of Middleburg, halting to rest for a few minutes on the outskirts. In passing through the village, a very neat little place, we were surprised at the number of Southern soldiers lining the streets. They exhibited a great deal of curiosity at our picturesque but ragged uniforms. They were wounded, sick and convalescent soldiers on furlough. As we passed out of the town we saw two men in front of a miserable looking dwelling. One was supporting his emaciated form on crutches, and appeared to be suffering not from sickness, but from a severe wound. One of the men in our ranks kindly enquired where he received his wound, and he answered "Bull Run."

November 7. It commenced snowing this morning shortly after we resumed our march and continued until about three o'clock this afternoon. The men grumbled, expressing a wish that those at home who clamored so loudly for a winter campaign had to carry a heavy knapsack through the cold storm, and were bitter toward Horace Greeley and James Gordon Bennett whom they considered chief authors of their misery. They joked about Bonaparte's retreat from Moscow and Washington at Valley Forge as if our situation was really as bad as theirs.

November nine. We halted last night at White Plains and are now encamped in sight of Warrenton.

November ten, eighteen sixty-two. This morning, early, we were ordered to get ready for review and about eight o'clock we were drawn up in column by division on the road awaiting the reviewer. No one knew positively who was to be the reviewing general, but opinion was about equally divided between the army's favorite and Burnside. We were cautioned not to cheer without orders and quietly sat down in our places. Soon the thundering cannon began to belch forth a salute and cheer after cheer could be heard, dispelling all doubt, for we all knew that no other could create such a tumultuous furore of enthusiasm than little Mac. himself. The sounds approached nearer and louder and soon our favorite appeared at the top of the hill, riding eight or nine paces in advance of a large cavalcade of horsemen, bowing his uncovered head to his enthusiastic admirers. When I looked at the noble leader I felt for the first time in a long while a decided sensation of enthusiasm burning in the ashes of my defunct patriotism. The boys of the One Hundred and Fortieth Regiment tried to obey orders not to cheer, but were finally unable to restrain themselves any longer, so their pent up enthusiasm gave way, and a "spontaneous combustion" of cheers aiding us, resulted in a demonstration loud and long. Our enthusiasm was at its height, we were full and running over so that we did not notice the fact that we were not marched away as usual after he had passed, till the Adjutant, Lieutenant Guthrie, commanded "attention to orders" and commenced to read General Burnside's acceptance of the command of the Army of the Potomac. Uncertain rumors of this change had been circulating for several days but no one believed or was willing to believe them, so it was as if a clap of thunder had been heard from a clear and cloudless sky. The men looked at each other in amazement, and dissatisfaction was written on every face, for if, as I believe, they all admired Burnside, they certainly loved, nay, fairly idolized McClellan. What could be the meaning of it? Was he made Commander-in-Chief in Halleck's place? No, that was not mentioned. All sorts of speculation was rife and the only comfort we could get was to look forward to our release from the army. Six months more for me and I'll be free.

November eleven. Last night on evening parade McClellan's farewell address was read to his army The adjutant's voice trembled with emotion and officers and men were visibly affected.

The 5th New York drilling at the double-quick during the winter encampment near Falmouth. [Engraving by Edwin Forbes]

CHAPTER 26.

*Words of commendation; review by General Hooker;
promised promotion.*

November thirteen, eighteen sixty-two. The Prince de Joinville, son of King Louis Philippe of France, when he returned to Europe from the Peninsula, issued a small pamphlet on the American Rebellion, in which he singled out our former Colonel, now Brigadier-General Warren, as an example to prove the superiority of regularly educated West Point officers. I saw the article this morning in the Philadelphia Enquirer and was much pleased with the complimentary manner in which he spoke of our ci-devant Colonel and regiment. An extract of his pamphlet reads as follows: "Sometimes an officer of the regular army, desirous of distinguishing himself, and having enough influence in his state raised a regiment and obtained from it an admirable result. Thus a young Engineer Lieutenant named Warren, was marvelously successful with the Fifth New York Regiment of which he was Colonel. That regiment served as engineers and artillery at the siege of Yorktown, and having again become infantry, conducted itself as the most veteran troops at the battles of the Chickahominy, where it lost half of its force. And yet these were volunteers, but felt the knowledge and superiority of their chief."

For some reason or other we have not received our rations and the boys, hungry and grumbling, tell fabulous stories of capacious appetites and boast of their ability to swallow an ox or a pig or a sutler's wagon.

Corporal James Franklin of our company, who was wounded at Bull Run, returned yesterday to the regiment. The rations have arrived and never did sour bacon taste sweeter or hard crackers softer.

November sixteen. Evening parade was over and we, after listening to a long list of court-martial cases, were dismissed to our quarters. The men were assembling around the blazing company fires with their coffee cups, when a cheer, a loud, uproarious, hearty cheer, ascended from the throats of a group of Zouaves encircled around two or three horsemen. We could not distinguish their faces in the dusk but we learned who one of them was, in time to join in the second round of cheers. It was General Abram Duryee, our old Colonel, the first and best. We cheered him with a hearty good will. He professed himself and really appeared glad to see us. He said, "You have proved yourselves to be an honor to the city and state you came from." He also said, "The people of that city and state will proudly welcome you back and carry you in their arms." In the midst of another hearty cheer he rode smilingly away toward the tent of General Warren, evidently well pleased with the warm welcome he had received from his old troops.

Our arms were inspected this morning and the articles of war were read. There is divine service in the camp to which the boys are respectfully invited to attend, but few avail themselves of it.

November seventeen. Brigadier-General Fitz John Porter, personal friend of McClellan, has been relieved from his command and sent home to stand trial for charges preferred against him by Major-General Pope. Major-General Joseph Hooker assumes command of Porter's corps which is now designated the Third or Central Grand Division of the Army of the Potomac.

We broke our camp and started forward in a drizzling rain this morning in the direction of Warrenton which is situated on the top of a hill from which the country can be seen for miles and miles around. It is a pretty country town, with neat and tasty houses. On top of the hill at the entrance to the town there is a large and elegant church with a tall steeple. It was just one o'clock when we entered the town by the clock on this edifice. About nine o'clock we reached Warrenton Junction where we found Hooker's old division snugly encamped. We could get no wood to build fires nor stakes to erect our tents and it was still raining.

November eighteen. No improvement in the weather today, it continued to rain and we continued to march from early morning till late at night. Our men were completely played out but not a man left the ranks, although many from other regiments lined the road.

November nineteen. We marched only four or five miles this morning and are now halting within fifteen miles of Fredericksburg.

November twenty. Weather still bad and no prospect of clearing. The camp is enveloped in the smoke of camp fires. Our ponchos and blankets are wet and our tents cold and cheerless. Our spirits are heavy like our wet clothes and "fellows of infinite jest of most excellent fancy" are dull and sluggish like the weather. Occasionally a grumble can be heard. Wanamaker wishes there was a peace convention to settle the matter. Brazzoni wants to go home. Cogswell threatens in the next fight to fire one volley and then skedaddle, and Mitchell fears we will never take Richmond.

November twenty-one. It rained incessantly again all last night and soaked through tents and blankets. I was submerged in water and wrapped in a saturated blanket, as cold as Iceland, and as uncomfortable in the watery element as a fish is out of it. I didn't sleep and was glad when daylight began to struggle with the darkness for I wanted to see the exact amount of misery I was in. When I emerged from the tent I felt like a person rescued from a watery death. My limbs were aching and stiff as the neck of a Pharisee, my voice was husky as Hamlet's dead daddy and my head and stomach were aching in sympathy.

The face of heaven this afternoon is again wreathed in smiles, the gloom-dispelling sun shines once more and the ground is rapidly drying. Cheerfulness has again resumed her sceptre and her loving subjects bask once more in the sunlight of her smiles. The boys outside are calling to their comrades to "come out of your hives and see the sun."

November twenty-two. We marched about four miles this morning, the weather being clear and cold.

November twenty-three. Moved forward again this morning, encamping about three miles further on. I was detailed to guard the ammunition train. The last wagon frequently got stuck in the mud, finally losing all trace of the rest of the train. We followed about three miles out of the way and returned to camp footsore and weary. The paper this morning reported the Confederates again in possession of Warrenton.

November twenty-four. When we crawled out of our tents this morning we found the ground covered with a heavy white frost, the air exceedingly cold and nipping and the noses of our comrades the color of live coals. It was cold, but not as cold as it will be, and we trembled with apprehension for the future.

November twenty-nine. We were reviewed this morning by General Hooker, a silver-haired old gentleman with white whiskers and severe look. Eighteen new recruits arrived today and John Peters has returned. Captain Wheeler has been assigned to the command of the company.

November thirty. We received new uniforms today.

December first. Captain Wheeler this afternoon, while I was drilling the recruits, drew me aside and informed me that he was thinking of making me a sergeant. I thanked him for the consideration but said that Caruthers was ahead of me on the list of corporals and was entitled to the promotion. He said he knew that but as two sergeants were to be made, his turn would come bye and bye. He said he expected to be very strict with his non-commissioned officers and wanted them to do their duty and he would do what was right with them.

December eighth. Days and weeks are quietly gliding away. They are sailing down the silvery stream of time, touching the snags that stud the stream of life. The mornings and evenings are cold, just now, the ground is covered with snow, but the glorious sun shines upon the earth, making the crystal carpet of winter sparkle with its light. God is good to His children. He smiles upon us through nature and we lift up our hearts in thankfulness to our Maker.

Oh! how many evidences there are that He still watches over our welfare, manifesting His goodness and love in many ways, notwithstanding our perverseness and ingratitude. Oh God, Almighty Father, illuminate my darkened heart with thy love and wisdom. Let the light of love shine in my selfish soul so that I may be able to fulfill Thy will. Let me never forget Thy goodness in the time of trouble and be forever more obedient to Thy will!

An unknown Duryée Zouave poses for a field photographer, possibly at the regimental winter camp on the Henry farm near Falmouth, Virginia, 1862-63. [Richard K. Tibbals Collection]

CHAPTER 27.

Fredericksburg.

December ninth, eighteen hundred and sixty-two. Major Winslow has been made Colonel, Captain Duryee, Major, and Sergeant Fish of Company B, Lieutenant and assigned to our company. Lieutenant Winslow was transferred from Company F to Company C. Last night, on recommendation of Captain Stephen W. Wheeler, I was promoted to sergeant.

December tenth. We are again under marching orders and may start tomorrow. Sixty rounds of cartridges are to be given out today, which looks like business. Nothing is definitely known as to our destination.

December eleventh. About half-past six o'clock this morning, just at daybreak, we were all ready to start, awaiting the call to "fall in," when the big bulldogs of war began to bark in the direction of Fredericksburg, causing great excitement in the camps of the new regiments, and dismay in the camps of the old. The One Hundred and Fortieth and the One Hundred and Forty-sixth, being green, received the news with a yell of satisfaction. Our men heard the news silently, for they knew what fighting was. There was only an occasional discharge at first, but the firing soon became more rapid and the battalion was ordered to "fall in." The red sun was just rising in the rosy east when we started and the ground was hard and white with frost. We passed General Hooker's headquarters and turned off on the road to Falmouth, halting for a few minutes in a wood. Here we could hear the noise of the big fellows, barking away with savage fury, and the rumbling growl that accompanied them, and when we resumed our march we could hear the hissing, snappish snarl. Further along we discovered at the top of a hill a long new embankment of earth, with cannon in position, the gunners lounging around. We halted in a little ravine, stacked arms, and unslung our knapsacks. We sat down on them, scarcely getting comfortable before a terrific cannonade began on the left and continued without intermission for about fifteen minutes, a rattling, roaring, crashing chorus of artillery above anything I have heard except the same instruments of death at Malvern Hill. The undisciplined soldiers rushed to the top of the hill to witness the performance, while the imperturbable Fifth lounged quietly down in the mud to sleep, as the ground was rapidly thawing. I was aroused by someone exclaiming "The city's on fire!" I followed him to the hilltop and could see the city, with three churches ornamented with steeples, in plain view. A house near by was on fire, burning brightly. The smoke curled up in great volumes around the church steeples, sometimes concealing them from view, again clearing away to show them still untouched. The city is situated in a valley with a background of dark, hazy-looking hills. The chimney tops and the steeples can be seen with the white wreaths of shells bursting around them. Away off to the left is a little hill, but not so insignificant as it looks, for the gunners on that hill have the biggest guns and they are the most busy in the destruction of the city.

December eleven, eighteen sixty-two. At two o'clock in the afternoon the doomed city was on fire in four different places, the red sheets of flame devouring the homesteads of the poor and the palatial residences of the rich alike.

December thirteen, eighteen hundred and sixty-two. A thick, smoky fog hangs over our camp this morning and hides Fredericksburg from our view. The boys are busy cooking their steaks and some of them like myself have already finished breakfast. They are noisy and sing songs, a certain sign that they have "slept the night well" and are feeling fine and merry. No noisy cannon has yet awakened the god of war from his slumbers and a strange, unnatural stillness reigns around. A report is in circulation that the enemy cavalry is in our rear. I secretly hope they will stay there without approaching nearer, but I fear the existing stillness is "the calm that precedes the storm." There is no knowing in time of war "what a day may bring forth," but I hope it will bring forth another mild night of sweet repose. We shall see. About nine o'clock the sun peeped through the clouds to see how matters stood below and the fog began to skedaddle from the face of the ground. Some movement had been going on in the fog and the result was a heavy cannonade on the left apparently across the river. The sound of the guns was dull and heavy at first, deadened, probably, by the density of the atmosphere, but soon grew lighter as the air got clearer and it became evident from the sound that a heavy artillery fight was in progress. Heretofore we have had all the artillery firing to ourselves, but today Johnny Reb is at work replying. Our muskets have been inspected and we are all ready for the engagement. The weather is mild and the boys cheerful. They listen complacently to the sound and appear to be indifferent alike to danger or excitement. The railroad is working briskly between here and Aquia Creek, and the sound of the steam whistle can be heard at intervals in the roar of the battle. Horsemen are riding to and fro, teams are passing and teamsters swearing, and occasionally the clear notes of the bugle can be heard around the camp.

The artillery had continued about an hour when the musketry fire began sounding like fire-crackers in the distance.

About two o'clock a pale, thin man with a sharp, keen eye and a quick, nervous manner rode up to the colonel of the One Hundred and Fortieth to deliver some order. The pale man was Brigadier-General Gouvernour R. Warren. No one heard the order except him for whose ear it was intended, but everyone knew instinctively what it was and began accordingly to prepare for an advance by buckling on his accoutrements. The colonel who received the order has an extraordinary and warlike name, O'Rourke, which suggests Irish chivalry. He has an austere look and a deep, monotonous voice. After receiving the order he rode out in front of his battalion and delivered the order of "attention" in a drawly sing-song manner as if singing the Doxology. The battalion falls in and so does ours, the One Hundred and Forty-sixth and the Regulars, the bugle sounds the order "forward" and off we start in the direction of the city, defiling over the hills and streams, through the mud, for the ground has softened in the sun. After we crossed the brow of the first hill, we could see the city quite distinctly, also the Confederate earthworks around it. On the right there is a formidable earthwork with heavy guns in position, but the guns were silent and the battery apparently deserted. The guns of the battery we had just left and those of another Federal battery on the banks of the river directly in front of the city were vigorously engaged in shelling this work. We halted behind the battery I have mentioned and witnessed the bombardment of the Confederate fort. The city is situated on a little hill that slopes to the water's edge, the banks of which being higher on this side afford an excellent view of the city. Back of the city on a ridge of hills are the Confederate batteries. We can see the smoke arising from them at every discharge, for they are now firing rapidly, and occasionally through the smoke we can see the sun glistening on the brass pieces. A shot from one of their pieces strikes the ground near us but does no damage. They have discovered our position. The noise of the musketry is very distinct as if the fighting was going on in the streets. The battalion is about to move forward again and I shall be compelled to put up my notes for the present. The boys want to know if I am the reporter for the "Daily Bladder."

The Rappahannock at Fredericksburg is a shallow and narrow stream. We crossed on a pontoon bridge of boats covered with heavy planks. Both boats and planks are splintered with shot and riddled with holes, made by the enemy sharpshooters on the opposite bank when our men were constructing the bridge. I have no ambition to become a pontoon bridge builder after such a positive proof of their dexterity with the rifle. The bridge was a very unsteady concern oscillating from side to side beneath our heavy tread, causing us to stagger as if drunk. I was really afraid of getting sea sick and didn't like the idea of losing the coffee I drank just before we started. On the opposite side of the river some soldiers guarding the bridge were boiling their coffee, the bullets whistling through the streets and the big balls crashing through the houses, but these soldiers were undismayed, apparently more concerned about their coffee than their lives. They were seated on cane-bottomed chairs, a luxury that a soldier doesn't often indulge in, and appeared to be exceedingly comfortable and happy. The homes of the city were filled with holes and shattered with shot. I had an idea that a cannon ball would bring down a house, but it forces its way through and leaves a hole, or else rips off a single board which it smashes to smithereens, and if built of brick it knocks out two or three as dexterously as a prizefighter does the teeth of his antagonist and leaves a little more ragged-looking hole than it does in a board. Striking a chimney it brings it down entirely, therefore there are few chimneys left in Fredericksburg. The furniture of the houses seemed to suffer more than the houses themselves. It was scattered around the streets in miscellaneous confusion, tables without legs, stoves without feet, chairs without backs and bottles without necks. We passed through Caroline Street and turned to the right in the direction of the firing.

The streets were full of soldiers, the stores were broken, the contents scattered around. The city was larger than I had anticipated, with large, elegant brick edifices beautifully laid out and tastefully ornamented with balconies, piazzas, colonnades and verandas. There were spacious gardens attached to almost every home and handsome trellis-work arbors. The balconies and colonnades were lacerated with shell and the gardens ploughed up with shot. Streets were wide and regularly laid out in blocks, through which we passed rapidly, and reached the suburbs.

Armed bodies of disciplined troops were moving to and fro and batteries of artillery moving to the rear. Solid shot was passing through the deserted houses, shells were bursting in the air over our heads and bullets whistling around our ears. The troops moving to the rear looked cheerful and smiled, those moving to the front looked serious and frowned. Wounded men were staggering through the streets to the hospitals, of which there were many, but none too many, notwithstanding every other house was occupied for that purpose, yet all seemed to be full. The little pieces of red flannel that fluttered from the windows and doors were no protection to the unhappy inmates, for the cruel balls at enmity with brick and board made no distinction, demolishing alike hospitals and deserted dwellings that lay in their way.

Immediately back of the city there is a gently sloping hill, with here and there an isolated house; immediately back of this hill there is another, Marye's Heights. On the brow of this hill the Confederate batteries were planted with the guns directed toward the city, and at the foot of the hill on the top of the slope mentioned there was a line of rifle pits and a stone wall surrounding a clump of bushes and trees and a barn. Behind this stone wall the enemy sharpshooters were posted with the muzzles of their deadly rifles peeping through holes, through which they could fire in perfect safety upon our troops.

The stone wall was a formidable defense and our troops after being twice repulsed during the day lay flat upon the ground in front. The sharpshooters were skillful and at every discharge from their unerring rifles the soul of a Federal patriot ascended to his Maker. The least movement was equivalent to certain death.

When we reached the scene of the conflict it was quite dark, for the sun was setting when we entered the city, and the position of the enemy could only be inferred by the sheets of flame that belched occasionally from the mouths of the guns.

We drew up in line of battle in a turnip garden behind a high board fence. The ground was soft and sticky and our feet were buried in the yielding clay. We tore down the boards of the fence and used them for a platform to stand upon. The One Hundred and Fortieth was directly in front and the One Hundred and Forty-sixth to our rear. We could see the flashing of the musketry two or three hundred yards in front and hear bullets whistle past our ears and we expected every moment to press forward and take an active part in the fray.

When we halted in this position the firing was disconnected, but soon became more rapid and fierce, for the rebels had emerged in the darkness from their hiding places and were making a vigorous assault upon our forces in front. Our troops were slowly pressed back, and the enemy having obtained its object, again returned to the shelter of its stone wall and rifle pits, leaving the dead and wounded to welter in their blood upon the field. After this there was only an occasional discharge and the troops prepared to pass the night upon the field.

The fence accommodated a great many of our boys and the rest went in search of boards in the rear. Captain Montgomery accepted my place on the fence and I started off with the rest toward the house behind us, but I hadn't proceeded a hundred yards when a solid shot went screaming through the air over my head and passed completely through the house. I relinquished my design upon the house and started toward the stable, and one standing near said, "There's chickens in there." I asked why he didn't go in and get one and his answer was, "I don't want to walk over the dead men." Again I changed my mind and ripped off a board from a fence to lie upon. I lay down but was unable to sleep, for loud and clear above the deep breathing of sleeping comrades I could hear sounds more fearful than the screeching of the shells and more melancholy than the sighing wind; sounds to "make wolves howl and penetrate the breast of even angry bears." It made my blood curdle to hear. They were the cries of the wounded, long and piteous wails of agony, mingled with plaintive cries and deep goans of despairing misery. Occasionally a piercing shriek broke upon the air, and cries of "Help! help!" or "Water!" My heart ached for the poor helpless sufferers but we were unable to help them for no one dared to stir to aid these poor fellows, for the Confederates were on the watch with their murderous rifles, ready cocked, making a target of every shadow that moved. I tried to shut out the sound with the end of my blanket. My thoughts were busy and I wondered if God's ears were open to the fearful cries of agony. One poor fellow, delirious, no doubt, was continually calling for "Charlie!" "Charlie!" but the only response to his wild and fearful cry was the crack of a rifle or the thundering report of a gun. "Oh! Oh! Oh!" was the cry the whole night through and I was glad when daylight began to break over the scene of death.

December fourteen, eighteen sixty-two. The god of day had not yet risen in the east when we arose from our beds of boards. No one waited to be called but all arose spontaneously and began silently to prepare for the day's work. Not a word was spoken above a whisper. Everything was silent as death. Dusky figures moved stealthily around in the dim, uncertain light of the breaking dawn and the One Hundred and Fortieth moved slowly away like a mist before us. The One Hundred Forty-sixth followed immediately behind them and our battery was left alone upon the field. On our left was a muddy street and deep in the mud lay some objects that appeared like bundles of old clothes. As the sky began to brighten these bundles began to assume a more distinct appearance. Could it be possible they were some of the men of the regiments which had just left, still lying asleep? A comrade shakes them but they do not stir, for they are dead patriots embedded in the mud and covered with glory. One lay on his hands and knees with face half buried in the mire, while others were stretched out with arms extended. It was a sickening sight. I don't know which I esteem the most offensive, the sounds of the preceding night or the sight of this morning. I have looked upon death, but nothing has equalled the horrible appearance of a mutilated hero on the battlefield, covered with dirt, begrimed with powder, half buried in the mud.

About fifteen or twenty minutes after the other regiments had taken their departure, we started off and marched by the right flank back to the street and down toward the river. The enemy battery on the hill, in order to show they were not asleep, sent their compliments in the shape of a shell. We ascended a little hill and reached the summit, when another one burst, scattering fragments in every direction. They were getting the range beautifully when we turned to the left into a lot between two houses, just in time to avoid the third shot, which went whistling down the street we had just left, just as the last group was passing through the opening in the picket fence. The house on the right of this hill belongs to a man named Carmichael, a politician. The house directly opposite, the enemy is using for a target. Sitting on a heap of knapsacks I can see the battle field and the rebel batteries. Their position is well known but the earthworks around appear as nothing but heaps of unpacked earth hastily thrown up to conceal the gunners. Although not visible, they are there, for every once in awhile an iron messenger of death starts forward on its mission of destruction. If a tree stands in its way it is splintered, and the irresistible ball continues its journey, lopping off heads and limbs of men and horses in its mad and spiteful career, gradually diminishing speed till it strikes the ground, where it rolls into the gutter. The masses of infantry, when they hear these reports, bow down their heads, horsemen bend forward on the necks of their chargers, the wounded cringe and wince, and isolated soldiers and stragglers dodge behind trees. We cannot return the fire for we can get no available position for our artillery, all the hills being occupied by the enemy except the one where we are stationed, and a battery of artillery could never maintain itself there for a moment under the heavy fire of the enemy's works.

Our troops are lying in three distinct lines on the slope of the hill, the first close to a little ravine that crosses the field, close to the stone wall, the second a little below, and the third at the foot of the slope. Not a movement could be seen along the first line, not a man has stirred, not a head nor an arm nor a leg has moved. I afterward ascertained that they were all dead, some killed, no doubt, in the charge of the preceding day, but far the greater number had been butchered where they lay by the concealed Confederates in the houses and behind the stone wall. They had been exposed needlessly to a terrible fire, for they were unnecessarily close to the rebel works. They died more like martyrs than like soldiers, for they had arms in their hands but were unable to use them.

Individuals in the second line showed signs of animation by firing occasionally but the least movement was followed by a dozen shots from the stone wall and almost every shot was sent with fearful certainty into the body of the daring soldier who fearlessly exposed himself. The wounded were unable to leave the field and their comrades were unable to help them, for the enemy fired upon everyone who stirred, making no distinction between the wounded and those who were not. Many poor fellows, already maimed, were shot down while endeavoring to leave the field and many received wounds, in their noble efforts to help their injured comrades. It was a fearful scene of death and slaughter, for the enemy handled its pieces with consummate skill, aiming with fearful accuracy. It was not a battle, for a battle is a conflict in which some injury is inflicted by victors and vanquished. It was nothing but needless slaughter. The third line of Federal troops, being less exposed, suffered less and some of the wounded succeeded in hobbling from the field while others were carried off on stretchers. One of the stretchers stopped. The face of the man on it was concealed by the cape of his coat. There was a rigidity about him which caused the carriers to feel his pulse and heart, which had ceased to beat. They laid the warm corpse beside a cold one lying near and returned to the battlefield with the blood-stained stretcher.

We had had nothing to eat except hard crackers and raw pork since arriving in Fredericksburg. The salty pork made us thirsty but the building of fires was strictly prohibited. Coffee was an indispensable luxury and must be had at all hazards. Some went into near-by houses, some made small fires of paper and some like myself dug holes in the ground and boiled coffee on the light of candles.

About two o'clock in the afternoon a Brigadier-General rode carelessly out to the end of the street and scrutinized the position of the contending forces. There was an expression of anxiety on his face.. It was General Griffin. He was followed by a single attendant. About three o'clock our position was discovered and immediately the iron began to fall around us very earnestly. We had to change our base to a garden in the rear of a house where we were permitted to boil coffee on the kitchen stove and soon began to feel quite comfortable. Some of the boys while prowling around discovered some flour, and flapjacks were on the bill of fare for the evening and were in great demand. The supply was equal to the demand, however, and three or four hundred extraordinary appetites were appeased. Our troops were still lying in the field prone in front of the enemy and nothing had been gained. For thirty hours they had remained there upon the field, losing a man a minute, nearly. They were unable to move, to eat or drink, without jeopardizing life or limb, and not a single inch of ground had been won in all that time from our vigilant and active foe.

December fifteen, eighteen sixty-two. Today in our regiment has been a day of unparalleled gloom and despondency, a day of doubt and fear. Brave men who never faltered in the discharge of duty are seen shaking their heads in hopeless despair and conversing in cautious whispers. Burnside is fearlessly criticized and the whole movement openly pronounced a terrible failure. There is a perfect dread of the hill where our troops are lying and a feeling of terror seems to animate every breast at the mere mention of it. The idea of our being called upon to relieve the troops there is received with unspeakable horror. Everyone looks aghast at the idea of charging the enemy works and horrible stories of blood and slaughter find eager listeners. This state of feeling has been produced by various causes. First, it is manifest that we cannot carry the rebel position and could not hold it if we could get possession, for there is a second line of defenses stronger and more formidable than the first. Second, is the obvious hopelessness of ever reaching Richmond by the Fredericksburg route, for there are four additional rivers to cross between the Rappahannock and the Confederate capital, the North Anna, the South Anna, the Mattapony and the fatal Chickahominy. The roads are in bad condition and the natural defences are said to be strong along the entire route. With all these insurmountable obstacles in our way, independent of a desperate foe to contend with, we plainly see the stupendous folly and wonder at the quixotic schemes of our General. This has a disheartening effect, but the helpless appearance of our men upon the field contributes mostly to the present demoralization of the army. The activity of the enemy, firing at every moving thing, is considered to be further proof of our inability and their confidence. It is exceedingly dangerous to procure water and the men detailed to that duty when they are marched off look as if they are going to their own funerals. About one o'clock a volley was fired and shortly afterward a regiment of Pennsylvanians, color bearer and all, came rushing down the street in perfect panic. The colonel, sword in hand, was vainly endeavoring to rally the men. It was the most disgraceful affair I had witnessed during the war. Just at dark our fears reached a crisis, for it was rumored with a pretty fair show of probability that we were to take our turn on the field that night, and the men were lugubriously discussing the perils of the situation in little groups of three or four. It was feared that the town was being evacuated, for we could distinctly hear the muffled wheels of the artillery moving away, and the idea of being left alone, unaided, to cover the retreat of the army from the city of the dead, was terrifying. I am not superstitious, but a strong feeling took possession of me that I was near the spirit world. I was not the only one troubled with forebodings, for Chicken Webb, who is by no means chicken-hearted, informed me that he believed he was about to croak, and the lion-hearted Tiebout was afraid the march to the hill would be last he would make. About seven o'clock in the evening a volley of musketry and a few scattering shots were heard remarkably close and the excited men rushed frantically to their arms without an order and grasped their haversacks. About half-past seven we were ordered to "get ready" and at eight we were halting in the street awaiting orders. There were two or three battalions in the street beside us, and some were armed with picks and shovels. Our regiment was divided into companies and dispatched in different directions. My company and Company I were sent under charge of the major in the direction of the rebel batteries. Silently and stealthily we marched past the place where we halted yesterday and slowly and cautiously we descended the hill; a cat could hardly walk more noiselessly. Dead men were lying in the road and the mild weather made them smell to heaven. Quietly we moved on to the foot of the hill, where the outline of the rebel batteries could be seen with terrible distinctness, although the night was dark, and Massacre Hill, replete with horrors, lay directly on the left. Life or death seemed to depend upon the way we turned and, thank heaven, we turned to the right. A man rose up from the ground in the darkness and enquired "Who comes there?" The major responded and the man approached the company. He was a picket and we had come to relieve him and his companions. I never saw a man so overjoyed before. He told us in broken, disconnected whispers that the enemy had, during the day, driven his regiment across the ravine and killed a great many of his comrades. They were unable to bring away the wounded and their loss was unknown. He concluded by advising us to "lay low" and "keep quiet" and above everything else not to show our heads a foot from the ground during the day.

We were posted at intervals along the edge of a ravine and left there on our stomachs to contemplate at leisure the precariousness of our situation. We understood we were to remain there twenty-four hours, a very pleasant prospect. I had Morrissy on one side and Cleary on the other. Cleary was in a dilemma; the boys had resolved that if ever they were conducted to Slaughter Hill, to remove their caps, for they had heard that the red fez of the Zouave was a splendid mark. Cleary had a red head, and the unfortunate brick-top didn't know what to do, as he was afraid it wouldn't make much difference whether he removed his cap or not. He sorrowfully remarked, "My head would be red, anyhow." He consoled himself by saying, "I can only die once." We had not been long on our posts before we could distinctly hear the sound of something like the clatter of a steel scabbard. It was made by a pick. The enemy was busy, no doubt strengthening his works, for the grating sound of shovels could likewise be heard in the stillness of the night. The sound proceeded apparently from behind a tree, directly in front of Morrissy and me. There were several houses which, we were told, were filled with the enemy. After we had been about an hour on the ground we were provided with picks and shovels and told to dig pits for ourselves. We were instructed by Captain Wheeler how to dig them and how to bank up the earth on the outside to protect us from a fire of grape and canister, which the rebels would give us for breakfast in the morning. We never worked more earnestly in our lives. The pits were to accommodate two men and Morrissy and I went into partnership, one watching while the other dug. If a man looks intently at a stump or stone in the darkness it will gradually assume some horrible shape. Morrissy had been looking at something he thought was a Confederate, the most horrible apparition that his mind could conceive. He bawled out excitedly for me to "git down," and "git down" I did in the dirt I was digging, with considerable celerity. Later he joyfully announced that it was "all right."

We were not disturbed in our labors except by an occasional rifle shot and we successfully completed the work. When the pits were finished we moved into them quietly and awaited coming events. At midnight it began to rain furiously, a cold, chilling rain that made us shiver, and we felt very miserable in our muddy pits for they were rapidly filling with water. They were too narrow to turn around in so we had to remain in one position with the water pouring down our backs. I never felt so uncomfortable since the night that preceded the battle of Hanover Court House.

About half-past three in the morning Lieutenant Fish passed our pits and told us in an almost inaudible whisper to "get ready." He didn't say for what and we were left with our minds tossing on the turbulent sea of uncertainty. All that I had read about blood-thirsty pirates telling their unfortunate victims to "get ready" passed through my mind, and I remembered how ministers and doctors made use of these ominous words to their trembling hearers lying on the verge of eternity. The Confederates, perhaps, were about to make a charge upon the pits and we were to get ready to receive them. The officer returned along by the pits and again whispered, "Put on your knapsacks." The sharp crack of a rifle followed the words and a bullet whistled in the air over our heads from the tree in front; a second and a third quickly following made it evident that our vigilant enemy was making a target of our brave Lieutenant. If they could see him they would see us when we emerged, as the last command established the fact we were about to do beyond the possibility of a doubt. We had no time to consider the question, for the captain was already moving toward us and withdrawing the men. It was a very strange proceeding, for there were none relieving us and we were deserting the position and the pits we had dug, and stranger still, the Confederates did not fire at us. We turned off down toward the city, where we were joined by two other companies. The whole movement was enveloped in mystery as profound and incomprehensible as the Egyptian sphinx. There was a hill in this street beyond which there was an embankment of new earth in the form of a quarter-circle. This embankment explained the whole movement, for it was a shallow and unsubstantial affair, incapable of making the slightest resistance to either shot or shell. It was situated so as to look formidable and was merely thrown up during the night, as a blind, to deceive the enemy with a show of strength while we evacuated the city. Our surmise of the preceding night was correct, for we were covering the retreat of the army and this frail scarecrow of a barrier along with the empty pits were to cover ours in turn. To get past the obstruction without knocking down the loose dirt, we were obliged to pass through a store filled with empty flour barrels. We passed through a side door and came out at the front, joining the main body of the regiment, which we found drawn up in line behind the barrier. It was now almost daylight and we could plainly read the name of the grocer, I. W. Alexander, on the sign over the door. We remained near the barrier till broad daylight and then removed to the first street below, from which we could see part of the enemy's battery. Bullets began to whistle around us pretty lively, making us hasten till we got in front of Slaughter's store on the bank of the river. We halted long enough for the lines to close up, after which we continued our retreat and soon reached the pontoon bridges, the sight of which had an exhilarating effect, and all breathed more freely on reaching the opposite bank. We felt as if we had escaped from some loathesome dungeon and every man felt a gleam of joy to turn his back on "Burnside's slaughterhouse."

General Warren was the last to cross the river.

CHAPTER 28

Christmas, eighteen sixty-two, and the new year, in which I am discharged.

December sixteen. This morning we returned to our old camp which we left on the morning of the eleventh. In passing the spot where we bivouacked the first two days, I turned instinctively in the direction of the fatal city. I expected to see the Confederate flag waving from one of the church steeples, but none was to be seen and the city looked so quiet and was reposing so peacefully on the banks of the Rappahannock that the last three days seemed like a dream.

December seventeen. An order was read off this morning from General Sykes complimenting the First Regular and the Fifth Regiment for their soldierly conduct in covering the retreat of the army from Fredericksburg.

December twenty-fifth, eighteen sixty-two. I was sent in charge of a brigade detail to the division hospital to dig trenches and draw wood. Four men, victims of the winter's campaign, had died there the preceding night and we buried them this morning. They were buried in their blankets and the heavy earth gave back a dull, unpleasant sound as it fell upon their breasts. This was the way I passed my Christmas day.

January first, eighteen hundred sixty-three. The old year and its stirring events have passed away. It is written in letters of blood upon the tablets of time and nothing has been gained by the Federal Government. Our enemies are bold and confident, for they are flushed with victory, while we, on the contrary, are discouraged and crippled with defeat. We have organized armies large enough to amaze the world, which have been worsted upon many a bloody field. While thinking of these things I heard the voice of the sergeant-major outside calling for a sergeant and two privates for guard in heavy marching orders immediately. It being my turn I could not evade the order and accordingly began to get ready. The drum sounded and the guard began to fall in. I was ordered to conduct the detail to Stoneman's Switch and report there for duty, where I was to receive further orders from the Assistant Adjutant-General, Captain Marvine. He was standing in front of General Warren's headquarters when I marched up my detail. I halted them at a respectful distance. When about to report I was intercepted by an orderly who handed me a slip of paper which was the verbal instruction in writing. Stoneman's Switch was on the railroad (switches usually are), but upon what particular part I was yet to ascertain. I understood my duty too well to ask my superiors any silly questions and I started off, trusting to luck, which led me several miles out of the way to the intense disgust of my comrades. We found the place, however, and were placed over some of the quartermaster's stores, where we are to remain three days.

January fourth. A man from another regiment joined our little circle around the fire last night. He said he had seen our regiment in Baltimore and lavished praises on our officers and men. He belonged to the first regiment of cavalry that crossed the Potomac and had been discharged for disability and was returning home with the body of a friend, and we assisted him on the cars with his burden.

January sixth. "Some of the best generals in the army," says the Herald of the fifth, "have expressed much solicitude in regard to the regiments whose two year terms of service expire next April or May. The first thirty-eight regiments from the state of New York will go out of service in May and among these are some of the best regiments in the army. It is deemed important by our best military authorities in the field that the best material in the rank and file and the officers of such regiments should be induced to remain." This paragraph afforded much amusement. The men laughed and the word "inducement" became a byword.

January seventh. In consequence of the weather this morning being colder than usual, we thought we would escape battalion drill, but alas! for human hopes and expectations, ours were doomed to disappointment. Our piratical-looking Colonel, who loves "pride, pomp and circumstance" of glorious display, had us out in spite of the cold, without overcoats, too, to shiver through the distasteful drill. The men wanted to know whether the drill was one of the "inducements."

The papers today confirmed the reports of the western victories, but they were dearly bought, the battle of Murfreesboro costing the Federal troops the loss of nineteen colonels, nine thousand men, seven thousand prisoners and twenty-eight cannon. The evening was cold enough to freeze the brains of a brass monkey, but we were drummed out half naked; however, we almost forgot our own suffering when we saw the colonel rubbing his ears. It afforded us a great deal of satisfaction and savage joy to know that he felt the cold too.

January eight. Our regiment has reason to be thankful, for at present we are free from sickness, while the men in other regiments are carried to their last resting places in the little graveyard on the hill in front of Henry's house. A number of naked little mounds on some bleak hill constitutes the soldiers' cemetery. No fence around, no weeping willow spreads its drooping branches over them. They lie in regular rows of eight or ten, quietly sleeping, and there they will continue to lie long after the little mounds are beaten down, till the last trumpet call of the resurrection sounds the reveille of life eternal.

We were reviewed this morning by Major-General Ambrose E. Burnside. It was a formal affair and took place on the Falmouth road about five minutes' march from the camp, but the colonel in marching back took the wrong road and led us about five miles out of the way. Mike Wimmer, without any disparagement to Cooper, thinks he deserves the title of "Pathfinder."

January nineteen. The fever of uncertainty that preceded all army movements is now raging in our camp with unparalleled fury. We have been under marching orders for the last week but no one can figure where we are to go.

January twenty. We began to think the movement had been abandoned, but about ten o'clock we heard a distant trumpet sound the call to "strike tents" and we were soon ordered to get ready by one o'clock. The order stated that "the enemy had been weakened on the Rappahannock by the movements of Foster in North Carolina and the brilliant achievements of the armies in the west and it was only necessary to follow up these victories and with the aid of Divine Providence crush the terrible rebellion." Before night the rain descended and our progress on the muddy roads became necessarily very slow. The wagons, the artillery and the pontoon trains got stuck in the mud and we bivouacked in the woods.

January twenty-one. We moved about five miles during the day, when the whole army got stuck in the mud. It rained throughout the whole day.

January twenty-two. It still continued to rain and it is therefore impossible to move. It takes twelve mules to drag one caisson. The men are more disgusted than ever and desertions from the different regiments are alarming.

We are to cross at Bank's Ford. Johnny is already there with his cannon planted to dispute our passage of the river.

January twenty-three. A large detachment went out yesterday to build corduroy roads through the mud.

February two. We have quietly settled down again in our old camp. We are waiting for our new General, Hooker, who succeeded Burnside Jan. 26, 1863. We go out to drill every day and march around the camp like the Israelites around Jericho.

February three. A bitter cold morning with snow. Off on picket. Major Duryee in command of troops, whose lips are blue with cold. Intensely cold evening.

February fourth. More snow.

February fifth. I relieve a picket, snow dissolves to rain, terrible night, no sleep.

February sixth. Another stormy day, no relief, no grub, no patience.

February eight. The first funeral in the regiment for some time; death from exposure on picket duty.

February thirteen. Colonel Winslow has returned from a ten days' furlough to New York. He has gotten himself up in the very best style, regardless of expense.

March twenty-fifth. Men were refused egress from camp this afternoon as on evening parade orders were read that information had been received that the enemy was approaching, warning the men to be in readiness to fall in at a moment's notice and ordering the camp guards under no consideration to leave the quarters of the guard.

May fourteen, eighteen sixty-three. Having served my two-year enlistment, I received my discharge today. It was signed by Captain Stephen W. Wheeler.

As this is simply my own personal experience and by no means a history of the war, my narrative ends here, but I am filled with thankfulness that the Army of the Potomac and its officers went on to victory and honor in the remaining years of the rebellion.

—FINIS—

Officers at the Segar House near Camp Hamilton, 1861. Left to right: Major Davies, Lieutenant Colonel Warren (with telescope), Assistant Surgeon Martin, unknown sentry, Chaplain Winslow (at table), Adjutant Hamblin, Colonel Duryée and Surgeon Gilbert. [Brian C. Pohanka Collection]

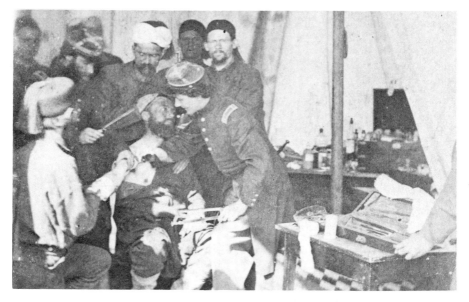

Wearing their officers' uniforms, Surgeon Rufus Gilbert and Assistant Surgeon B. Ellis Martin recreate an operation on a "wounded" Zouave at Camp Hamilton. [Brian C. Pohanka Collection]

120

Rev. Dr. Gordon Winslow (left), the patriarchal fighting Chaplain of the Duryée Zouaves. [New York State Archives] Judson Kilpatrick (right), a "pony" like Southwick, joined the unit as Captain of Company H through the influence of G. K. Warren. At Big Bethel, Kilpatrick inflicted the only Confederate fatality and was himself wounded in the thigh. [Patrick A. Schroeder Collection]

Duryée's Zouaves drilling in camp near Fort Monroe, 1861. Note the white havelock is worn beneath the fez. [From a sketch by Thomas Nast]

The charge of the Duryée Zouaves at Big Bethel, June 10, 1861. [From a sketch by Thomas Nast]

Captain Cleveland Winslow (left), eldest son of Rev. Dr. Gordon Winslow, was a dashing but unpopular officer who was Colonel of the 5th New York at its muster-out in 1863. [Mass. MOLLUS, U.S. Military History Inst.] Gordon Winslow, Jr. (right) served with his father and brother in the 5th New York, attained the rank of Lieutenant, and later served as Captain in the 5th Veteran Volunteers and as a staff officer for Major General G. K. Warren. [New York State Archives]

Private Frederick G. Smart (left) of Company B stands guard outside the battlements of Fort Federal Hill, Baltimore. Smart was severely wounded at Second Bull Run. [Robert T. Martie Collection] An unidentified Corporal (right) of the 5th New York at Federal Hill. Since he carries a Sharps Rifle, he is a member of either Company E or I -- the unit's flank and skirmish companies. [Richard K. Tibbals Collection]

First Lieutenant Thomas W. Cartwright (left), Company G, 5th New York. Wounded in the right shoulder by a shell fragment at Gaines's Mill, Cartwright died from the effects of his wound on December 26, 1862. [New York Division of Military and Naval Affairs] Captain George L. Guthrie (right) of Company H. He commenced his wartime service as Corporal, served as Regimental Adjutant, and later became Lieutenant Colonel of the 5th Veteran Volunteers. [Patrick A. Schroeder Collection]

Felix Agnus

Born 1839 in Lyons, France. Agnus served as a sailor on a French merchant vessel, and as a soldier in the 3rd Regiment of Zouaves before coming to America in 1860. He was working as a sculptor at Tiffany's jewelry store when he enrolled as a Sgt. in Co. H, 5th N.Y. He was 5'9", with a light complexion, and weighed 140 pounds. As 2nd Lt., Agnus was severely wounded in the right shoulder at the battle of Gaines's Mill. Following his recovery he served as Major and later Col. of the 165th N.Y., or "Second Battalion, Duryée Zouaves." By the war's end he was a Brevet Brig. General. In later years, Agnus was owner and editor the <u>Baltimore American</u> newspaper and a powerful force in Maryland politics. He died in Baltimore on October 31, 1925.

Carlile Boyd

A native of Scotland, Boyd was 33 years old when he enlisted as 2nd Lt. of Co. F. As Capt. and acting field officer, he was severely wounded at the battle of Second Bull Run, losing two fingers on his right hand, as well as being struck in the left thigh, left arm and side. Major of the 5th N.Y. at the regiment's muster-out, Boyd later served as Col. of the 14th Regiment Veteran Reserve Corps. Following the war he continued in the Regular Army as Capt. in the 44th and 17th U.S. Infantry. He retired in 1879 due to ill health and alcoholism. Boyd died in Germantown, PA, March 22, 1883.

John Henry Brown

Enlisted in Co. F, April 29, 1861, at age 21. Served as orderly in Stewart Hospital, Baltimore. Promoted Sgt. in July 1862, he was reduced to the ranks four months later. Brown died in Philadelphia, 1891.

John H. Carroll

Born in England of Irish parents in 1837; he came to America in 1855. Enrolled in Co. E, April 23, 1861; a bricklayer and milkman, 5'4", with blue eyes, brown hair and dark complexion. Known as a fine singer and a practical joker, Carroll was captured at Second Bull Run while serving as Color Cpl. Following his parole he attained the rank of Sgt., and was mustered out with the unit in May 1863. He died April 4, 1900.

William H. Carothers

Enrolled as Pvt. in Co. F, April 21, 1861. He was a 26-year-old saddle and harness maker by profession. A steady soldier, he rose to the rank of 1st Cpl., and both he and Southwick were promoted Sgt. on Dec. 8, 1862. After the war, chronic eye problems eventually left him nearly blind. He died in Moundsville, WV, October 31, 1919.

Thomas W. Cartwright

This 19-year-old clerk enrolled as Pvt. in Co. G, April 25, 1861. He received a wound in the thigh at the battle of Big Bethel, and rose through the ranks to 1st Sgt., and 2nd Lieutenant. A strict and sometimes cruel disciplinarian, Cartwright's nickname among the enlisted men was "the fiend." As 1st Lt., at the battle of Gaines's Mill he was severely wounded in the right shoulder by a shell fragment. Infection claimed his life six months later, Dec. 26, 1862. Cartwright's father and brother both served as officers in the famed "Irish Brigade."

Jeremiah Cleary

Born in Ireland and a printer by profession, Cleary enrolled at age 18 as Pvt. in Co. F, August 20, 1862. He was 5'5 1/2", with blue eyes, auburn hair and a light complexion. Cleary deserted Dec. 26, 1862.

Julius Cogswell

Enrolled as Pvt. in Co. F, April 23, 1861. He was a 23-year-old clerk, 5' 8", with blue eyes, brown hair and dark complexion. Nicknamed "Bingo," his mischievous antics and happy-go-lucky nature made him a well known regimental character. Taken ill on the infamous "Mud March" in Jan. 1863, Cogswell served out his time with the 5th N.Y., but never fully recovered. He died of consumption Aug. 9, 1882, at the age of 45.

Henry E. Davies, Jr.

Born July 2, 1836, to a prominent New York family. He was a practicing lawyer when mustered in with the regiment as Capt. of Co. C. In August, 1861, Davies left the unit to become Major of the 2nd N.Y. Cavalry. By war's end he commanded a division in the Army of the Potomac's Cavalry Corps, and attained the rank of Major General. He died in Middleboro, MA, Sept. 7, 1894.

J. Mansfield Davies
Age 32 at his muster-in, he was the first Major of the 5th N.Y., and like his cousin, Henry E. Davies, left the unit to accept a commission in the 2nd N.Y. Cavalry. Davies served as Col. commanding the 2nd N.Y. Cavalry. until Dec. 1862, when he was succeeded in command by another former Duryée Zouave, Judson Kilpatrick.

Simon Deely
Enrolled at age 21 as Pvt. in Co. F, July 16, 1861. He was killed in battle at Gaines's Mill, June 27, 1862.

George Duryea
The elder brother of Hiram Duryea, he joined the 5th N.Y. at age 30, as 1st Lt. of Co. E. As Capt. of Co. C he was severely wounded in the left groin at the battle of Gaines's Mill. Suffering from constant pain and occasional paralysis, he returned to the regiment and was promoted Major and then Lt. Col. in Dec. 1862. George Duryea was despised by many of the enlisted men for his harsh discipline and habit of beating supposed shirkers with the flat of his sword. He never fully recovered from his wound and died April 1, 1897.

Hiram Duryea
Born in Manhasset, NY, April 12, 1834. He was a distant cousin of Abram Duryée and entered the 5th N.Y. as Capt. of Co. E. With pre-war service in the State Militia, Hiram and several of his brothers worked with their father in the management of a profitable starch manufactory at Glen Cove, Long Island. He was 5'71/2", with brown eyes, brown hair and dark complexion. Nicknamed "Black and Tan," he was a strict and sometimes arbitrary disciplinarian. But he was a driving force in transforming the Zouaves into a proud and well-drilled unit. As Lt. Col., Duryea led the regiment in the Seven Days battles, and as Col. commanded the 5th until fever contracted on the Peninsula

compelled his resignation in Nov. 1862. Brevetted Brig. Gen. for his gallantry at Gaines's Mill, he played a prominent role in the post-war Veterans Association. He was murdered by his deranged son, Chester B. Duryea, on May 5, 1914.

Abram Duryée
Born April 29, 1815, in New York City, of French Huguenot ancestry, he was the founder and first Colonel of the 5th N.Y. A wealthy mahogany importer and Manhattan businessman, Duryée was for more than a decade commander of the elite 7th N.Y. State Militia. Having witnessed the drill of Elmer Ellsworth's Zouave Cadets in 1860, at the outbreak of war Duryée determined to outfit the 5th N.Y. -- initially called the Advance Guard -- in full French Zouave regalia. In fact Abram Duryée did not long command the unit that would bear his name. Exercising brigade command as early as June 1861, in September he was promoted to the rank of Brig. Gen. and left the Zouaves. Wounded at Second Manassas and Antietam, he resigned from service in Jan. 1863. In his post-war career he served as New York Police Commissioner and Dockmaster, but suffered severe financial reverses. He died from complications following a stroke September 27, 1890.

John F. Farrell
Born in 1828. Employed in a paper store, he had gray eyes, dark brown hair, a fair complexion and stood 5'61/2", and enrolled as a Pvt. in Co. F, April 24, 1861. Farrell suffered a severe wound in the right thigh at Second Bull Run. He was promoted Cpl. and later served in the 146th N.Y. and the Regular U.S. Army (1867-75). Farrell was a member of the New York Fire Deptment when he died, Aug. 13, 1884.

Thomas E. Fish
A 27-year-old printer, he enrolled as Pvt. in Co. B, April 25, 1861. Fish rose through the ranks to 1st Lt. of Co. I, served as Acting Adjutant in early 1863, then joined the staff of Gen. Warren as Inspector General. He died in Rochester, NY, in 1868.

Charles Fortesque

A 23-year-old machinist and native of New York. At the outbreak of war he was working for a railroad in Tennessee. Fortesque enrolled as Cpl. in Co. F, April 24, 1861. He stood 5'7", with blue eyes, light hair, and a light complexion. Promoted Sgt. in Oct. 1861, he was absent sick from the summer of 1862 through May 1863. Fortesque died at the Ohio Soldiers Home, Dec. 27, 1923.

James H. Franklin

Born Nov. 26, 1833, and a resident of Yonkers. He enrolled as Pvt. in Co. F, Oct. 19, 1861. Franklin was 5'71/2", with blue eyes, brown hair and a light complexion. After promotion to Cpl. in July 1862, he was shot through the back of his right thigh at Second Bull Run. He returned to the unit in early 1863, and later served in the 146th NY. Franklin died in Jersey City, NJ, Oct. 4, 1923.

George L. Guthrie

Born in Ireland in 1833. He was employed as a clerk and bookkeeper when he enrolled as Pvt. in Co. D, April 25, 1861. Standing 5'11" and weighing 180 pounds, Guthrie rose to the rank of Sgt., served in the Color Guard at Gaines's Mill, and was promoted 1st Lt. and Acting Adjutant in Sept. 1862. At the regimental muster-out he was Capt. of Co. A. Guthrie later served as Capt. and Lt. Col. in the 5th N.Y. Veteran Volunteers. After the war, he suffered from chronic diarrhea and alcoholism. Guthrie died in New York, March 28, 1892.

George O. Hager

Boston-born, and a veteran of the California Gold Rush. He enrolled April 25, 1861, at age 31, as 1st Sgt. of Co. C. Promoted 1st Lt. of Co. F in Sept. 1861, and Capt. in Aug. 1862. Garbed in a new gold-braided jacket, before going into battle at Second Bull Run the Captain remarked, "Boys, won't I make a fine-looking corpse?" Hager perished in the fight and his body was never recovered, although his pistol turned up in Nashville, TN, in 1894.

Joseph E. Hamblin

Born in Massachusetts on Jan. 13, 1828. He worked in the insurance business in New York and was a member of the 7th Militia. Hamblin went west in the mid 1850s and played a part in the sectional troubles of "bleeding Kansas." Commissioned Adjutant of Duryée's 5th N.Y., the 6'4" Captain was one of the few officers who held the affection of the enlisted men. When he left the unit in Nov. 1861 to accept the rank of Major in the 65th N.Y., the men of the 5th presented him with a horse, "Zouave." By war's end Hamblin had attained the rank of Brig. Gen. He died July 3, 1870.

Thomas Healy

Born in Providence, RI, Aug. 31, 1842. Enrolled as a Pvt. in Co. F, July 16, 1861. He was 5'7", with blue eyes, light hair, a fair complexion, and by trade a blacksmith. Nicknamed "Whitey Bob." He was wounded in the right leg and left arm at Second Bull Run. Transferred to the 146th N.Y. with other 3-year men, Healy was captured at the battle of the Wilderness and confined at Andersonville, where he lost all his teeth to scurvy. He died at the National Soldiers Home, TN, Nov. 3, 1918.

Harmon D. Hull

Born in Fulton, Oswego County, NY. He was a member of the 7th N.Y. Militia. Enrolled at age 26 on April 25, 1861, as Capt. of Co. A. Promoted Major in Sept. 1861, Hull went on recruiting service at the conclusion of the Seven Days Battles. He held the rank of Lt. Col. when he resigned in Dec. 1862 to assume command of the 165th N.Y. (Second Battalion, Duryée Zouaves) though he never actually took the field with that eight-company battalion. Hull was active in the New York National Guard after the war as Col. of the 4th N.Y. "Veteran Zouaves." He died June 6, 1902.

Judson Kilpatrick

Born in Deckertown, NJ, on June 14, 1836, and a graduate of the May 1861 Class at West Point. Kilpatrick is best known as a daring and reckless Union cavalry general. He was also the first Capt. of Co. H,

5th N.Y., having been tendered that position through the intervention of G. K. Warren, a pre-war instructor at West Point. Wounded in the right thigh at the battle of Big Bethel, Kilpatrick tendered his resignation in Aug. 1861, to accept field rank in the 2nd N.Y. Cavalry. He rose steadily to brigade and division command, and attained the rank of Major General. Kilpatrick was United States Minister to Chile at the time of his death, Dec. 4, 1881.

George W. Leavitt
A native of Maine. At age 25, he enrolled as Pvt. in Co. F, on July 8, 1861. As Cpl., Leavitt was killed in action at Second Bull Run by a shot to the head.

Wilbur F. Lewis
Born in Ulster County, NY, the son of a Methodist Episcopal Minister. He enrolled April 25, 1861, as 1st Lt., Co. D, age 23. Promoted Capt., Lewis was an acting field officer when killed in action at Second Bull Run. Shot from the saddle of "Black Jack," Hiram Duryea's former warhorse, his foot caught in the stirrup and the terrified animal dragged his body over the field. His brothers Frederick and Edward also served with the Zouaves; Fred was wounded at Gaines's Mill, and Edward was killed at Second Bull Run.

James Mahoney
Born in Ireland, Nov. 1842. Standing 5'83/4", he enrolled as Pvt. in Co. F, April 29, 1861. Shot through the right side at Gaines's Mill, Mahoney recovered and was promoted Cpl. in Dec. 1862. He died Jan. 24, 1912.

William H. Mandeville
Born Nov. 11, 1833, and a resident of Fordham, NY. He enrolled as Pvt. in Co. F, April 25, 1861. Nicknamed "Harry," he served for a time as clerk at Brigade Headquarters. He was struck twice in the chest and killed 30 yards from the enemy lines at Gaines's Mill, June 27, 1862.

Effingham W. Marsh
Enrolled as Pvt. in Co. F, April 25, 1861, at age 21. He stood 5'7" and was by occupation a clerk. Promoted Cpl. in Aug. 1861, and Sgt. in Jan. 1862. Wounded through both legs and in the left hand at Second Bull Run. Later served as 2nd Lt. in 145th N.Y. He died Oct. 10, 1898.

Charles F. Matthews
Enrolled as Pvt. in Co. F, April 25, 1861, at age 34. Matthews contracted fever on the Peninsula, and was discharged for disability in Nov. 1862, while serving as a wagoner.

Azor S. Marvin, Jr.
Born in Brooklyn, Oct. 30, 1825. He graduated from the College of the City of New York in 1846, and went west in the California Gold Rush. Marvin operated a bookstore in San Francisco, and traveled around the world 1854-58. After working as an accountant, he enrolled as Pvt. in Co. A, April 25, 1861, and served as "right guide" to the regiment. Transferred to Co. I and promoted Sgt. in Nov. 1861; 2nd Lt. Jan. 1862; 1st Lt. Aug. 1862; Capt. Dec. 1862. Marvin served on Col. Warren's staff in the Seven Days Battles and continued to function as brigade, division and corps staff officer through 1864. He died in Bensonhurst, NY, Aug. 5, 1899.

George A. Mitchell
A 22-year-old machinist from Yonkers, he enrolled as Sgt. in Co. F, April 20, 1861. He stood 5'9", with gray eyes, light hair and a light complexion. Promoted 1st Sgt. in Jan. 1862. Slightly wounded in left forearm at Gaines's Mill. At Second Bull Run he suffered a contusion on the left hip by a bullet that smashed his haversack. An active member of the 5th N.Y. Veterans Association, Mitchell filled the office of President. He died in Yonkers, Dec. 27, 1923.

Charles Montgomery
Born Dec. 5, 1831, to a prominent Rochester, New York family. He received his education at Geneva College and trained as a civil engineer.

Montgomery was working as a stockbroker when he enrolled as Cpl. in Co. A, April 25, 1861. Promoted 2nd Lt. of Co. C, Sept. 1861, and 1st Lt. in May 1862. He commanded Co. B in the battle of Gaines's Mill. As Capt. in command of Co. C at Second Bull Run, he was knocked unconscious by a grazing shot to the head and captured. Following his exchange Montgomery served until mustered out with the regiment as Capt. of Co. I. He later served as Capt. in the 5th N.Y. Veteran Volunteers and killed commanding that unit at the battle of Hatcher's Run, Feb. 5, 1865.

James Morrissey
Enrolled as Pvt. in Co. F, April 22, 1861, at age 20. A carpenter by trade, he was 5'6", with gray eyes, brown hair and a ruddy complexion. In May 1861, his mother wrote to Col. Duryée asking that her son be sent home, as he was afflicted with "an immoral disease." Morrissey was shot through the neck and captured at Second Bull Run. Paroled, he recovered and served with the unit until its muster-out.

James Murphy
Born in Ireland and a resident of Yonkers. He enrolled as Pvt. in Co. F, May 9, 1861, at age 19. He was 5'8", with blue eyes, light hair and a light complexion, and a printer by occupation. During the Peninsula Campaign, Murphy fell ill with inflammatory rheumatism and was absent in the hospital from July 1862 to March 1863, when he rejoined the unit and was detailed as a company cook. He mustered out with the regiment. Murphy died Nov. 1, 1870, at Yonkers from the effects of his wartime illness.

Charles C. O'Neil
Enrolled as Pvt. in Co. F, July 16, 1861 at age 30. He was a bricklayer by trade. Killed in action at Gaines's Mill, June 27, 1862.

Leon Olivier
Enrolled as Cpl. in Co. B, April 25, 1861, at age 30. He made his living as a sculptor. A veteran of the French Army, he was proficient at the

bayonet exercise and helped to instruct the company. Olivier was killed at Gaines's Mill while serving in the regimental Color Guard.

Simon B. Parker
Enrolled as Pvt. in Co. K, April 25, 1861, at age 22. While serving as a Sgt. at Gaines's Mill, a wound to his right arm permanently disabled his hand. Promoted 2nd Lt., Co. D, Aug. 1862, and 1st Lt., Co. F, Sept. 1862. On recruiting duty in New York from Nov. 1862. Resigned in March 1863, and was discharged for disability April 22, 1863. He was one of the founders of the 5th N.Y. Veterans Association in 1866.

John Peters
Enrolled as Pvt. in Co. F, April 22, 1861, at age 23. Contracted fever on the Peninsula and absent sick from July to Nov. 1862. He received promotion to Cpl. in Dec. 1862. Mustered out with the regiment.

Edgar Phillips
Left his practice as a lawyer at age 24, to enlist as Pvt. in Co. F, April 25, 1861. Promoted Cpl., Aug. 1862, and Sgt., Jan. 1862. Shot through the neck and killed at Gaines's Mill.

Timothy Russell
Enrolled as Pvt. in Co. F, May 6, 1861, at age 21. He was 5'8", with gray eyes, light hair and a light complexion, and a ship's blacksmith by occupation. At Gaines's Mill, Russell was wounded in the groin and thigh, and the ring finger of his left hand was shot off. He received his discharge for disability on Nov. 15, 1862. Russell died April 14, 1889.

William C. Ryer
Enrolled as an 18-year-old Pvt. in Co. F on April 30, 1861. Promoted Cpl., Jan. 1862. Killed in action at Gaines's Mill.

Frederick W. Sovereign
Enrolled as Pvt. in Co. F, April 25, 1861, at age 20, he was a merchant

by profession. His father, Rev. Thomas Sovereign, was Chaplain of the 5th N.J. Infantry. Promoted Sgt., Aug. 1861; 2nd Lt., Jan. 1862; 1st Lt. and Adjutant, July 8, 1862. His nickname among the enlisted men was "Bull Head." Sovereign had recently rejoined the regiment from recruiting service when he was killed in action at Second Bull Run. While carrying Col. Warren's orders to retreat along the line, Sovereign was shot in the elbow and through the thighs, severing the arteries. His father located and buried the Adjutant's body during a truce, and later brought the remains home to Mt. Holly, NJ, for burial in the family plot.

Robert Stephenson
Enrolled as Pvt. in Co. F, July 16, 1861, age 26. Detailed as Hospital Steward in June 1862, and served in that capacity until he mustered out with the regiment.

Benjamin A. Sullivan
Born in London, England. At age 25, he enrolled as Pvt. in Co. F, April 30, 1861. A sign painter by trade, he was 5'3", with blue eyes, sandy hair and a florid complexion. Feisty, combative and mischievous, he became one of Southwick's closest companions. Sullivan was shot through the left side at Second Bull Run; the bullet fractured several ribs. Following a long period in hospital, during which he worked as a nurse, Sullivan was discharged for disability April 29, 1863.

Henry A. Swartwout
Born in Louisiana in 1834, he enrolled April 25, 1861, and served as the first Capt. of Co. F. Prior to the war he had been commandant of a military school in Maryland. Discharged to accept appointment as 1st Lt. in the 17th U.S. Infantry, Aug. 12, 1861. A Capt. and Brevet Major for wartime service, he died during a Yellow Fever epidemic at Galveston, TX, Oct. 8, 1867.

William Sweeney
Enrolled as Pvt. in Co. F, April 29, 1861, age 22. He was a gas-fitter by occupation. Mortally wounded at Gaines's Mill by a shot in the

thigh. He died from the effects of his wound and chronic diarrhea in a Philadelphia hospital, Aug. 10, 1862.

George H. Tiebout
A 35-year-old seaman, he enrolled as Pvt. in Co. A, May 9, 1861. Killed in action at Big Bethel, June 10, 1861, by a shot through the chest. He was the first man of the Duryée Zouaves to fall in battle. Shortly before his death he wrote, "Our regiment is called the red-legged devils, and.a terror to evil doers."

Samuel Tiebout
A 22-year-old clerk. He enrolled as Pvt. in Co. F, April 25, 1861. Promoted Cpl., Jan. 1862; Sgt., July 1862, and 2nd Lt., Feb. 1863. Severely bruised at Second Bull Run when a bullet smashed his canteen. One comrade called him "as good a soldier as I ever knew." Following the war Tiebout was employed as a bank teller and cashier. He died in Little Falls, NJ, April 8, 1889.

George W. Wannemacher
Born in Philadelphia, Feb. 8, 1841. A student, he enrolled at Baltimore as Pvt. in Co. C, Nov. 13, 1861. He stood 5'81/4", with hazel eyes, light hair and a fair complexion. Promoted Cpl. in March 1862 and Sgt. in May 1862. Struck three times at Second Bull Run, the bullets passing through both arms and his left hand. Promoted 2d Lt., Co. B, Sept. 1862 and 1st Lt., Co. I, Dec. 1862. Resigned due to disability on Dec. 29, 1863. Later served as Adjutant in the 40th Pennsylvania Militia. Following a career as a newspaperman, he died at the Soldiers Home, Los Angeles, CA, Dec. 23, 1925.

Gouverneur Kemble Warren
Famed as the hero of Little Round Top at Gettysburg, and as commander of both the II and V Corps, G. K. Warren commenced his Civil War service as Lt. Col. of the 5th N.Y. Born in Cold Spring, NY, Jan. 8, 1830, he graduated second in the West Point Class of 1850. As an Army Engineer he explored the Western territories and taught at the Military Academy before joining Duryée's regiment in April of 1861, as

second in command. On Sept. 11, 1861, he became Col. of the 5th N.Y. and assumed brigade command during the Peninsula Campaign. A strict but impartial disciplinarian, more than any other man Warren was responsible for transforming the Zouaves into a well-drilled fighting machine. Promoted Brig. Gen. in Sept. 1862, he became Chief Topographical Engineer under Gen. Hooker prior to the Chancellorsville Campaign. He died in Newport, RI, Aug. 8, 1882. Six years later the veterans of the 5th N.Y. erected a statue of Warren on Little Round Top at Gettysburg.

James L. Waugh
A 47-year-old restaurant owner, veteran of the 7th N.Y. Militia, and drillmaster for the Metropolitan Police, Waugh helped to organize the 5th N.Y. and became the first Capt. of Co. D, April 25, 1861. He resigned Aug. 10, 1861, following a disagreement with the regimental commander, G. K. Warren.

James W. Webb
Born in Brooklyn Sept. 2, 1841, and a hatter by trade, he enrolled as Pvt. in Co. F, July 1, 1861. He was 6'1", with gray eyes, brown hair and a dark complexion. In 1897 "Chicken" Webb was awarded a Medal of Honor for gallantry in action at Second Bull Run where he was slightly wounded while helping to save Hazlett's Battery from capture. Following service in the 146th N.Y., he ended the war as a Brevet Captain. After the war Webb traveled west, was a scout and lawman in Montana Territory, then returned to Brooklyn where he held a number of municipal offices. He was an active member of the 5th N.Y. Veterans Association and instrumental in the erection of the Warren statue at Gettysburg and the regimental monument at Second Bull Run. Webb died in Brooklyn, June 7, 1915.

Oliver Wetmore, Jr.
From a socially prominent New York family, and a graduate of Columbia University, he enrolled as 1st Lt. of Co. F, April 25, 1861, at age 26. Promoted Capt. in Sept. 1861. Afflicted with acute inflammatory rheumatism, he tendered his resignation June 18, 1862.

Wetmore later received a commission in the 19th U.S. Infantry, but was forced to resign in 1872 for being drunk on duty. He died April 5, 1873.

Stephen W. Wheeler

Born Aug. 28, 1833, in Richmond, NH. Enrolled as Cpl. in Co. A, April 25, 1861. He was 5'71/2", with blue eyes, brown hair and a light complexion. By profession Wheeler was a machinist and engineer. Promoted Sgt., Aug. 1861; Color Sgt., Sept. 1861; 1st Sgt., Dec. 1861; 2nd Lt. of Co. G, Feb. 1862; 1st Lt. of Co. C, July 1862; and Capt. of Co. F, Oct. 1862. He mustered out with the regiment. Later, Wheeler served as Capt. in the 25th N.Y. Cavalry and before the war's end received a commission in the 5th N.Y. Veteran Volunteers. After the war he worked for a cutlery company, and suffered from alcoholism and heart disease. He died July 25, 1907.

Michael Wimmer

Born in France, 1820. Abandoned his wife and son to enlist as Pvt. in Co. F at Baltimore, Oct. 24, 1861, at age 41. In Jan. 1863, he was detailed as clerk in the Quartermaster Department. When the two-year men went home, he continued to serve with the 146th N.Y. until his muster-out. Wimmer died of "excessive drink," May 31, 1872.

Cleveland Winslow

Born in Medford, MA, 1836, eldest son of Rev. Dr. Gordon Winslow, who served as Chaplain to the 5th N.Y. Employed as a clerk prior to the war, he enrolled as Capt. of Co. K, April 25, 1861. Transferred to Co. E, Sept. 1861; Major, Sept. 30, 1862; and Col., Dec. 1862. Brave, of striking appearance and fond of colorful uniforms, he was also a military martinet, whose almost fanatical insistence on order and discipline gained him the enmity of the men in the ranks. He was nicknamed "Lord Winslow" or "Garibaldi", and often characterized as a "tyrant" and "military despot" by those serving under him. After his muster-out, Winslow organized the 5th N.Y. Veteran Volunteers as a four-company battalion, which he commanded with the rank of Lt. Col. Following garrison duty in Alexandria, VA, the battalion joined

Warren's V Corps and was brought up to full regimental strength. Colonel Winslow was severely wounded by a shot to the left shoulder at the battle of Bethesda Church, June 2, 1864. He died of his wounds at Alexandria, on July 7, 1864.

Gordon Winslow, Sr.

Born at Williston, VT, Sept. 12, 1803. A graduate of Philipps Academy and Yale University, he attained a D.D. in 1833, and served as minister of the Congregational and later Episcopal Church. A resident of Staten Island from 1845, he served as Chaplain to the Quarantine, Pastor of St. Paul's Church, and was an amateur scientist, geologist and inventor. Prior to the outbreak of war he received a Doctorate in Medicine from New York University. Rev. Dr. Gordon Winslow was appointed Chaplain of the 5th N.Y. upon the regiment's organization and took an active part in all of the unit's campaigns and battles. He frequently served in a military capacity as an aide to G. K. Warren, and was also an agent of the Sanitary Commission -- a role he continued to play following the regiment's muster-out. A tall and patriarchal figure, with a flowing gray beard, Winslow was widely known throughout the Army of the Potomac. On June 7, 1864, he accidentally drowned when he fell from the hospital transport bearing his wounded son, Cleveland, to Alexandria. His body was never recovered.

Gordon Winslow, Jr.

Born in Elmira, NY, Aug. 30, 1838, younger brother of Cleveland and son of Gordon Winslow, Sr. He enrolled in the 5th N.Y. in Sept. 1862, and was appointed 2nd Lt. of Co. F. He was 5'8", with gray eyes, dark hair, and a light complexion. Promoted 1st Lt. of Co. C, Dec. 1862. He later served as 1st Lt. and Capt. in the 5th N.Y. Veteran Volunteers and as staff officer to Gen. Warren, commanding the V Corps. He entered the Regular U.S. Army in 1866, serving with the 15th, 33rd and 8th U.S. Infantry Regiments. Court-martialed several times for being drunk on duty, he was invariably reinstated, but suffered from alcoholism and intestinal illness. He retired from active duty in 1888, and resided in Berkeley, CA, frequently travelling abroad in an effort to improve his health. He died in Florence, Italy, Oct. 22, 1896.

Index to Southwick's Manuscript

Agnus, Felix Lt., 77
Alabama (steamer), 33, 36
Alexander, I. W., 114
Alice Price (steamboat), 20
Aquia Creek, VA, 87, 102
Astoria, NY, 32
Baltimore, MD, 46, 47, 66, 116
Bank's Ford, VA, 118
Bartow, Francis Col., 45
Beauregard, P. G. T. Gen. 44, 68, 69
Bee, Barnard E. Gen., 44
Bennett, James Gordon, 93
Berdan's Sharpshooters, 69
Big Bethel, VA, 41, 44, 48
Blackwell's Island, NY, 22, 32
Booth, John Wilkes, 48
Boyd, Carlile Capt., 27
Branch, L. O'B. Brig. Gen., 64
Brazzoni, Pvt., 97
Brown, John H. Pvt., 38, 39
Bull Run, 2nd Battle of, 88, 92, 95
Bull Run, 1st Battle of, 44, 45, 46
Burnside, Ambrose Gen., 45, 93, 94,
   110, 117, 118
Butler, Benjamin F. Gen., 39
Cambridge (steamer), 33
Camp Misery, 50
Camp Winfield Scott, 51
Camp Hamilton, 44, 46
Carroll, John Pvt., 32
Caroline Street (Fredericksburg, VA),
   104
Carothers, William H. Sgt., 92, 98
Cartwright, Thomas W. Lt., 51, 77
Cheeseman's Landing, 51
Chickahominy River, 65, 70, 80, 81, 83,
   95, 110
Cleary, Jeremiah Pvt., 112
Cogswell, Julius Pvt., 26, 27, 28, 97
Cold Harbor, VA, 58, 65, 73, 74

Commodore (hospital ship), 52
Cumberland, VA, 57
Davies, Henry E., Jr., Capt., 43
Davies, J. Mansfield Maj., 19
Deely, Simon Pvt., 76
Deitzwaller, John Latham Comet, 87
Delaware Legion, 48
Dix, John A. Maj. Gen., 47
Duryea, Hiram Lt. Col., 62, 72, 75, 77,
   79, 80
Duryea, George Maj., 100, 118
Duryée, Abram Col., 17, 36, 42, 47, 96
Elder, Alexander Pvt., 15
Ellsworth, Elmer Col., 40
Falmouth, VA, 100, 117
Farrell, John Pvt., 79
Federal Hill, 46, 47, 48
Fish, Thomas E. Lt., 100
Ford's Theatre, 87
Fort Monroe, VA, 33, 34, 39, 46, 48, 50
Fort Schuyler, NY, 17, 19, 23, 29,
   31, 34
Fortesque, Charles Sgt., 60, 74
Foster, John G. Gen., 118
Franklin, William B. Gen., 55
Franklin, James H. Cpl., 95
Fredericksburg, VA, 58, 100, 101, 103,
   109, 110, 115
Gaines, Dr., 70
Gaines' Mill, VA, 72, 80, 86, 88
Greely, Horace, 93
Griffin, Charles Gen., 109
Grover's Theatre, 87
Groveton, VA, 88
Guthrie, George Lt., 93
Hager, George O. Capt., 91
Halleck, Henry Gen., 94
Hamblin, Joseph E. Capt., 29
Hampton Creek, 41
Hancock, Winfield S. Gen., 54

Hanover Court House, VA, 58, 60, 63, 113
Harpers Ferry, VA, 39, 91
Harrison's Landing, VA, 85
Hazlett, Charles E. Lt., 90
Healy, Thomas Pvt., 70
Heintzleman, Samuel Gen., 45
Hooker, Joseph Gen., 54, 95, 96, 98, 100, 118
Hull, Harmon D. Maj., 76
Jackson, James W., 40
James River, 84
Jamestown, VA, 87
Joinville, Prince de, 95
Kerrigan, James Col., 17
Kilpatrick, Hugh Judson Capt., 29, 39
Lee, Robert E. Gen., 57
Leavitt, George W. Pvt., 79
Lewis, Wilbur F. Capt., 82
Lincoln, Abraham, 44
Longstreet, James Gen., 54
Loudoun Valley, VA, 92,
Louisiana Tigers, 45
Lounsbury, James H. Lt., 91
Magruder, John B. Gen., 50
Mahoney, James Pvt., 79
Malvern Hill, VA, 82, 83
Mandeville, William H. Pvt., 77
Marsh, Effingham W. Sgt., 76
Martindale's Brigade, 69
Marye's Heights, 105
Matthews, Charles F. Pvt., 32, 73
Marvin, Azor S. Jr. Capt., 116
McClellan, Geo. B. Gen., 46, 50, 54, 55, 58, 65, 66, 67, 93, 94, 96
McDowell, Irvin Gen., 39, 44, 46, 58, 65
Merrimac, 50
Middleburg, VA, 92
Mitchell, Maggie, 87
Mitchell, George A. Sgt., 97
Montgomery, Charles Capt., 106
Morrissey, James Pvt., 112
Murphy, James Pvt., 43, 54, 55
Nelly Baker (mail boat), 52
New York Times, 51

Newport News, VA, 87
O'Neil, Charles Pvt., 77
O'Rorke, Patrick H. Col., 102
Olivier, Leon Cpl.,77
Parker, Simon B. Lt., 91
Patterson, Robert E. Gen., 39
Pennsylvania Avenue, 87
Peters, John Pvt., 98
Phelps, John Gen., 36
Philadelphia Inquirer, 95
Phillips, Edgar Sgt., 76
Pig Point, VA, 36
Pleasant Valley, MD, 91
Pocomoke River, 48
Pope, John Gen., 96
Porter, Fitz John Gen., 50, 69, 71, 74, 80, 81, 96
Potomac River, 87, 91, 116
Prim, Gen., 69
Rappahannock River, 103, 115, 118
Raymond, Professor, 38, 39
Rebecca of Pottstown, 86, 87
Regiments
    1st Connecticut Heavy Artillery, 52, 62, 65, 70
    1st Michigan Infantry, 69
    14th Brooklyn, 90
    1st New York Infantry, 90
    2nd New York Infantry, 41
    10th New York Infantry, McChesney's Zouaves, 15, 41, 68, 74, 88
    62nd New York Infantry, Anderson's Zouaves, 56
    104th New York Infantry, 93
    140th New York Infantry, 100, 102, 105, 107
    146th New York Infantry, 100, 102, 105, 107
    2nd Rhode Island Infantry, 44, 45
    1st US Regulars, 115
Richmond, VA, 97, 110
Rip Raps, 34
Ropers Meeting House, VA, 55
Russell, Timothy Pvt., 79
Ryer,William C. Cpl., 77
Savage Station, VA, 83

Segar, Joseph Col., 34, 35, 44
Shenandoah River, 91, 92
Shenandoah Valley, VA, 92
Ship Point, VA, 51
Snicker's Gap, VA, 92
Snickersville, VA, 91
Sovereign, Frederick W. Lt., 38, 51, 88
Stephenson, Robert Pvt., 55
Stoneman's Switch, VA, 116
Sudley's Ford, VA, 44
Sullivan, Benjamin Pvt., 27, 28, 56
Swartwout, Henry A. Capt., 25,27,39,
    47, 91
Sweeney, William Pvt., 80
Sykes, George Gen., 49, 65, 66, 69, 70,
    71, 80, 115
Tiebout, George H. Pvt., 43
Tiebout, Samuel Sgt., 24, 25, 77, 111
Tunstall's Station, VA, 57, 72
Tyler, Robert Gen., 45
US Regulars, 70, 102
Vixen (gunboat), 24
Wannemacher, George Sgt., 97
Warren, Gouverneur K. Col., Gen., 47,
    48, 55, 65, 69, 74, 75, 77, 78, 79, 80,
    84, 88, 91, 95, 96, 102, 114, 116
Warren's Brigade, 60
Warrenton Pike, 44
Warrenton, VA, 93, 96, 98
Warrenton Junction, VA, 96
Washington, DC, 87
Waugh, James L. Capt., 23
Webb, James W. Pvt., 111
Wetmore, Oliver Jr. Lt., 25, 47, 91
Wheeler, Stephen W. Lt., 47, 98, 100,
    112, 119
White House, VA, 57, 72
White Oak Swamp, VA, 83, 84
White Plains, VA, 93
Wide Awakes, 18
Wilken's Brewery, 15
Williamsburg, VA, 54, 55
Wilson, Billy, 17

Wilson's Small (hospital ship), 52
Wimmer, Michael Pvt., 117
Winslow, Cleveland Col., 29, 30, 91,
    100, 119
Winslow, Gordon Rev. Dr., 43
Winslow, Gordon, Jr., Lt., 91, 100
Winthrop, Theodore Maj., 43
Wood, Fernando, 33
Yorktown, VA, 48, 49, 50, 51, 52, 54,
    67, 87, 95